FROM BOOM TO GHOST TOWN

FROM BOOM TO GHOST TOWN

CORNUCOPIA, OREGON

Thomas Taylor Cook

ISBN-13: 978-1721229888
ISBN-10: 1721229884

"If you cry out, I might hear you on the wind
And if the mountains echo your love to me, wave your heart
And I'll be riding back again."

From the song "Spirit Rider," (the last) Johnny Cash album,
copyright Universal Records, 2017

Dedicated to:

Nanci, Eric, Eliza, Matt and Annee

Many thanks to:

Sara and Jeff Artley, Larry Bush, Paul Fitch, Kerry Gulick, Dave Imus, Ann Ingalls, David and Katheryn Moore, Bill Schuhle, Blair Sneddon, Bob Taylor, Dale Taylor, Galen West, Betty Willett, and the staff at Pine Valley Community Museum.

CONTENTS

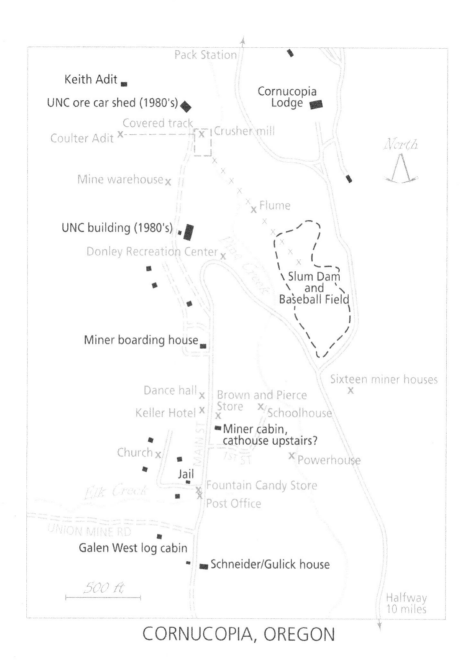

CORNUCOPIA, OREGON

X = vanished structure. ■ = existing structure. Some locations are approximate.

Most listed sites are private property. Please ask owner permission to visit.

Some historic and present locations are not listed, for the sake of map legibility and clarity.

Map courtesy of David Imus of Imus Geographics.

INTRODUCTION

*"You may see such....places, where only meadows and forest are visible –
and will find it hard to believe that there once stood...a flourishing little city
of two thousand souls....as in the old mining regions of California..."*

Mark Twain, *Roughing It*

WE LOVE GHOST TOWNS; THEY FUEL OUR IMAGINATION. A lot of imagination is required when visiting Cornucopia, if you are recreating the town at its heyday. Cornucopia, Oregon, is called a ghost town. The village is ranked from #1 to #3 on lists of the best Oregon ghost towns. We're not simply spectators while in a ghost town. We are players, exploring a village, using some real details, some created in our minds, recreating missing parts of the town.

It's hard to tell whether ghosts really exist, especially if you, like me, have never seen one. Perhaps one time I sensed an idea transmitted from a possible ghost. Bogus TV ghost shows make it even harder to believe. Reckon for yourself, of course, if the three Cornucopia and one Bourne area ghost tales presented here are pyrite or real gold. It's not hard to decide whether ghost towns exist. Ghost towns like Cornucopia provide settings for movies, novels, folk tales and tourism.

Ghost towns could be any historical town having evidence of previous glory. We examine a ghost town and dream of a once vibrant place. Ghost towns have not stopped being made in the west. In some rural areas, there are many small towns that have lately become ghost towns because nearly all or all business in town has closed. Then, residents started moving away. The new ghost towns are created due to many economic reasons. One of the causes of this trend is big box mega-stores in larger towns; within a radius of, say, 50 miles of the now ghostly town.

Examples exist of three kinds of ghost towns: deserted ghost towns, towns with a few people living there, and thriving ghost towns. In Cornucopia, now a few people live there year around. About a dozen weekend or summer houses dot the town. The year-round residents of Copia surely can feel the beginning of roots in their town. Though some of us are restless westerners, leaving a bust and seeking the next boom, there is still a human and cultural need for roots. We have a desire for at least a sense of the past.

Going back to 1880, there was no town at the present site of Copia, as the locals call Cornucopia. Instant cities, like gold mining boom towns, have not what we think of as history when they start. There is much history at each place. Native American and natural history go back thousands of years at Cornucopia. My book, *The Cornucopia: Oregon's Richest Gold Mine* has a focus on the Cornucopia Mining Company, the mine owners and the universe of the mine. In that book, I list local native tribes, some geological history, and ancient uses of the part of Pine Valley where the mine and the town of Copia eventually were located. Indigenous people did not generally think in terms of land ownership, until they were forced into that frame of mind by having to live on ever shrinking reservations.

The citizens of new cities have no time for history. They are busy building their town, and in a way, building themselves. Everyone at Cornucopia at the beginning of the town was an Argonaut, a sojourner, a newcomer. They survived, changing the environment to meet their needs. The citizens of Cornucopia must have been thinking of themselves as, really, from somewhere else. Copia grew without much planning. Once the town was platted, one could cheaply buy a lot and build without any permits.

The 'movers and shakers' of early Copia were not very prescient. Had they been, they surely would have set aside land for a town park or a cemetery. Planners also would have made sure that their streets and right of ways were defined and protected by civic deeds. This oversight is causing problems in Cornucopia, today. Despite the omissions and missteps, the town founders worked very hard to create the village.

Oregon gold miner work ethic reflects favorably on the whole of the American temperament. Tenacity, courage, resourcefulness, self-starting, teamwork, and improvisation were all reflected in the citizens of Copia. Because of these traits, when some children left Copia, many became highly skilled professionals.

After the town was founded, babies born in Copia were literally from there. Bob Taylor, he and his family discussed later, was the last baby born in Copia. Bob was born in a log cabin in Copia in 1941. In the future, if a tourist gives birth while staying at the lodge or in a vacation cabin, an event not soon to occur, Bob's 'last baby' status will be gone. Very few people alive today can accurately say they are from Copia. All of us that live in, work or visit Copia can still state we are from Copia. When we finish our latest visit to Cornucopia, at the moment we leave we are literally from Cornucopia.

Our individual view of history tends to diminish the reality of what really happened. To lesson that effect, many sources for this book are utilized: the 'thanks' paragraph, the footnotes and the references list. Of primary importance are interviews with a few of the people who lived in Copia, and can remember what the mining town was like during a boom time, prior to the mine's closure in 1941. We also get an accurate view of the deterioration, the bust phase of the town from the people who lived, most part time, in Cornucopia during the 1950's and 1960's.

A complete chronological history of Copia does not exist. This book will not serve as a guidebook, or complete history of the town. There are many individual years in the history of Copia where no historical examples can be found to relate. There are building sites that have totally reverted to forest land, with no trace of what was once there.

The earliest date of arrival at Copia, amongst the citizens interviewed for this book, is 1934. This year was the beginning of a boom cycle. A fictional visit to the town has been created in 1915. This was used as a device to portray what very likely were the sights, sounds and smells of the town of Cornucopia at its peak. Baker County voting trends and records are used as a way to delve into the moral and political thinking of the early day citizens of Copia. U.S. Census data has also been used as a research source.

Other sources: The Pine Valley Community Museum has nearly

as much original historical material on Cornucopia as the University of Oregon's Knight Library Copia archive possesses. Both collections, together, equal about five boxes of wonderful and sometimes boring material that anyone can study. These archives are like a giant pirate gold treasure map. Lots of unknown mysterious symbols, and once in a great while, X marks the spot!

In the 1970's, I bought a collection of over 800 papers from Cornucopia Mines in an antique shop. Some were illegible and with scorched edges, indicating that after the mine closed, there was a fire in the mine office. Kerry Gulick (more about him later) informed me that vandals burned down the mine office and one other building in the 1970's. One or two of these 1930's and 1940's Cornucopia Mine records, mostly 3"by 5" miner time cards and purchase orders, were inserted into each volume of my Cornucopia Mine book sold at the Pine Valley Community Museum. The first book, as this one, serves as a fundraiser for the museum's preservation efforts in Cornucopia.

After studying the 800 Copia mine papers, I'm keeping about 100 single mine records from the original collection, needed for book documentation. In case you bought the earlier book and are wondering 'where's my Cornucopia Mines antique paper at the end of the new book?' Sorry, they are now nearly all given away with each earlier book.

You can print your own ephemera about Copia, except the paper won't be authentic old Cornucopia Mines paper. Since the first book, more records pertaining to Copia are now being made available on line. The Oregon Department of Geology and Minerals, articles from the *Baker City Herald* and the State of Oregon History Archives have all added many new pages about Copia and the mine. An even better way to study Copia is to visit in person.

What's left at Copia is a relatively undisturbed village of over a dozen, spread out, original buildings, all pre-1941. Copia is so unlike commercially recreated mining ghost towns: Virginia City, Nevada and Columbia, California, where costumed actors and mining period costumed retailers affect our imagination. The lack of development at Cornucopia allows us to create for ourselves an uninfluenced, earlier world.

History and geography can unify us. Clearly, Cornucopians were very independent minded, yet strongly connected to all of Pine Valley. How a landscape looks, why it looked the way it did, combined and compared with how and why it looks like it does now are important. We give historical Copia a voice, now that most who remember the town are gone. Cornucopia is a signpost showing the way to the past, yet still with a future. I hope this book is rewarding for those who love the back roads of history and cultural geography.

Let's visit Copia, late 1940's and early 1950's, through the tales of former Cornucopia resident Blair Sneddon, early frequent visitor and sometimes resident Galen West. The 4th of July was one of the two big celebrations held in town each year.

CHAPTER 1
FIREWORKS AND AMERICAN PIE

"Peaches in the summertime, apples in the fall....."

"Shady Grove" – American traditional ballad

KA-BOOM!!!!! TWO CASES OF DYNAMITE – FIRED ALL AT ONCE – making a mighty ear ringing roar that echoed all around Pine Valley. The explosion was on the 4th of July, right in the gold mining town of Cornucopia. A grand, grand fireworks finale occurred, indeed. The explosion rocked the rocks and rocked the gold in the rocks. The explosion went off on an area leveled by years of spread out layers of gold mine mill waste.

There are microscopic bits of gold in the ground, right in this former fireworks and baseball area. About 5% to 10% of this particular ground consists of tiny rocks and slurry that contain tiny bits of gold. 90% is the best gold recovery rate, from rough ore, at the end of the 1930's gold ore milling process.

Mixed in the ground, there, are nearby Baker Mine mill wastes, and Union Mine mill wastes. They were reworked and reprocessed at the new Copia Mine mill, recovering 30 to 40% of the gold lost during the older, inefficient milling process. With the then new 1930's floatation milling process, the gold recovery efficiency rate significantly increased.[1]

At midnight, the Fourth of July celebration fireworks show grand finales occurred in the nearly ghost town of Copia. Throughout this book the town name Cornucopia, and 'Copia' will be interchangeable. Fourth of July has been heartily celebrated since the late 1880's in Copia, as was Labor Day. A smaller Christmas Party was put on by the mine for the village's children.

In the period 1942 to the early 1950's, Charley Sneddon, Blair's father, was the leader of the last three full time employees. They were the caretakers of Cornucopia Mines, after the mines shut down in 1941. Charley knew his dynamite well. He put together and lit off the big blast grand finale. We don't know if both cases of dynamite that were set off were full cases, or not. With the steep cliffs of Granite rock around, the fireworks echoes would have provided an extremely loud report.

Several of Galen West's family members had worked in Cornucopia Mines. At the time of the celebration described, his family was living down near Halfway. The Wests traveled north, up to the remote village of Copia, for the big party. It was a splendid place to have a celebration. At the time, locals called the mountains the Granites, generally not the Wallowas.

The mountains were both. In the clear mountain air, the Milky Way was very visible in the night sky at the town's elevation of about 4,800 to 5,000 feet. The town elevation varied depending on where you were standing in the steep sided glacial valley. A town party was going on.

After mine closure, the big Fourth of July celebration was on and near the flat mine waste area of the Slum Dam in Copia. Previously, there was also part of the Fourth of July celebrations in downtown Copia. The Slum Dam was not a dam as we know it. It was a mine mill waste area, on the east side of Pine Creek, across the creek from the Coulter adit (tunnel) and 1930's mine mill of Cornucopia Mines. Where the mine adit and mill were located, uphill from town on the west side of Pine Creek, there was not enough flat ground to store all the mine waste. The town has some buildable flat ground, but mostly in the Pine Creek flood plain.

A flume, looking like a thin railroad trestle, was installed from the bottom of the mine mill to cross Pine Creek. The waste traveled first by flowing water and gravity to a building that contained a small pumping station on the east side of Pine Creek. Then, the slum was pumped up to the 'dam' area, somewhat flat, about 2 acres, also on the east side of Pine Creek. At the lowest point of the Slum Dam area, the waste pile was reported to be up to 70 feet high. The mine moved the end of the mill waste flume from area to area, to spread out the slum. Part of the future Slum Dam area had been worked, as a 1912 Labor Day celebrations photo shows, to form a baseball diamond.

This flat area was where the 4th of July fireworks occurred. In the late 1940's, bulldozers and tracked scoopers had started removing the higher parts of the slum dam, dumping it into dump trucks. These workings leveled much of the 2+ acre slum dam area. The mine mill waste was later recycled for use as a gravel-sand mixture to truck to and mix with concrete for the new Snake River dams that were being built in the 1950's and 60's.

The Slum Dam mine waste was also used as gravel to repair seasonal damage to the road between Halfway and Copia. Don't dig here for gold. It's against federal environmental law to dig, signage states this. A two foot layer of dirt and rock sits on top to keep mine waste from leaching into Pine Creek.[2]

After digging for impossible-to-find gold, the gold will be in pieces smaller than the eye can see. Plus, after breaking the law, you would need a massive amount of money to build and operate a small state of the art gold ore processing plant to recover the very tiny amounts of gold left. Refining costs would far, far exceed the value of any gold you might, or probably not, find. In any case, the fireworks did truly 'rock' the gold left in the ground.

By the time of the party, late 1940's to early 1950's, it had been at least six years since the mine shut down. Except where the waste was recently removed and recycled, forest duff and debris from trees carpeted some of the Slum Dam. It was clearly the best place in Copia to safely hold a fireworks show; the largest bare and empty of trees and bushes flat clearing near the town. No one wanted to start a forest fire. The show was on mine-owned private land. This was, indeed, the Wild West.

Wild, yet the people of Copia 'policed' themselves quite well. I'm told that the county sheriff only made it up to Copia one or two times in the nearly 50 years of the town's active life. One time, the Sheriff came to gather trial evidence against robber Six Shooter Carnahan. This tale is told later. At the time of this vignette, folks were more concerned about the celebration, food, and beauty of the fireworks; illegal or legal.

Blair Sneddon[1] indicated his father would go to a far end of the

Slum Dam area, for safety's sake away from the crowd, to blow up the boxes of dynamite for the grand finale. The sticks of dynamite were surplus from the 1930's Cornucopia Mines cement powder house, still standing about 200 yards north from the mine entrance. This small, empty structure is on private land, not open to the public.

People living in Copia during the operation of the mine were used to hearing occasional dynamite explosions for mining near the surface, stump removal, or for road building. Explosions and fireworks can be dangerous, injuring many people each Fourth of July. No injuries were reported during the years of the Copia fireworks shows.

There were still a few people living and celebrating in Copia, since the mine stopped operations in 1941.[2] The Fourth of July party and fireworks show brought many up from the town of Halfway, 10 miles away, making a reported crowd of more than 50. We know, from historic photos, that Copia had a Fourth of July celebration yearly since early in the town's history.

Even after the mine closed, Charley and his wife Rhoda Sneddon invited everyone nearby to come to Copia for the celebration. Copia still had a reputation as a 'good times town.' A good time was had by all, indeed, for the Fourth of July parties. Blair states that cooks from Halfway restaurants, and others from Halfway, Richland and Copia provided tasty dishes to share. By the final years of the fireworks shows, the last restaurant and last grocery store in Copia had closed down.

Charley Sneddon's son Blair couldn't wait for dark when fireworks would begin. Blair tells me that fireworks were individually provided by local kids, each lit their own fireworks show for everyone to see. Most of the fireworks were bought in Halfway: small rockets, firecrackers, bottle rockets and other fireworks that mainly are now illegal in most cities in Oregon.

Galen West tells of three homemade fireworks sales stands in Halfway. Local junior entrepreneurs would gather roadside bottles and sell the bottles for profit, to buy the fireworks for their show in Copia. The fireworks, unlike today, were cheap. Five or ten cents would buy a pack of firecrackers. Cars were parked at the edge of the road at the Slum Dam, some leaving their headlights on so the kids could see, up on the slum dam, to put on their fireworks shows. The children at Copia painted the sky that night.

Blair indicates that the waiting for darkness was eased because of the tasty smorgasbord dinner. Whole tables of local, delicious homemade pies were laid out for the Fourth of July celebrants to partake from: Gooseberry, apple, rhubarb, mincemeat, strawberry and more. Early July was too early for Pine Valley picked wild huckleberry pie.

Some of the fruit used for Copia party pies came from the strawberry farm near Copia, more certainly from farms in Eagle and Pine Valley. There are, to this day, many local farms near Richland, New Bridge and Halfway that have orchards, most within twenty miles, downhill from Copia. In addition to the historical 'farm to table' flow of fresh fruit to the residents of Copia, local area fruit was and still is exported to many cities in the west. The local farmer's fresh fruit must have made outstanding pies.

There are four historical photos in The Baker County Library archives of strawberry farming in Copia. Strawberries were the only fruit, besides Huckleberries, that would grow at that altitude. All four Copia historical farm photos appear to be different views of the same Panter family strawberry farm.

None of this currently popular pie was served at Copia Fourth of July parties: big city factory-made, frozen, cardboard crust and awash with high fructose corn syrup. Once sliced, this fake pie oozes like an ocean of goo with some fruit and hard to pronounce chemical ingredients. Pie box graphics, for such a culinary monstrosity, often include a false Pine Valley-like farm image of a beautiful, old timey bucolic fruit orchard.

The food served at the Copia party was likely healthy and local, except perhaps the hot dogs. Potato salad, pickles and hamburger would have had local ingredients. The Fourth of July meal was served below the Slum Dam in a nearby picnic area next to Pine Creek, where a fine bright bonfire roared.

Chris and Jesse Schneider were part of the Fourth of July celebrations for many years. From the late 1940's, Jesse made pastry and coffee to serve free to the few tourists coming to Copia, even on a drop in basis. After economic reasons and then World War II caused mine shut down, Chris left Copia for a while, working in a mine near Kellogg, Idaho. Returning to Copia around 1946, Chris worked as a mine caretaker, later part-time. Chris had the distinction of being the person who worked the longest of all employees for Cornucopia

Mines, nearly 70 years.

Copia resident Ann Marker (Ingalls) states, that for safety, her father would not let her attend the slum dam fireworks show. Ann could still see much of it from the front porch of their Copia house.

Celebrations like the Fourth of July, Christmas and Labor Day were all very important to the residents of Copia, in an era before the entertainment of television or even local radio availability. The citizens of Copia, in both the early times and later, would get together, plan and put on festive holiday parties.

Imagine, in your mind's eye, an image of a quintessential holiday event in America; it's likely you will come up with a Fourth of July, flags and fireworks in a small town. Look at any of the Disneyland Park Main Streets. At the center of all the nearly identical old time Main Streets are early 1900's frontier style buildings going up just two stories. There are fireworks (unlike Copia, fireworks every evening). Seem familiar?

The largest celebration in Copia was the Labor Day party, followed closely by Fourth of July. At both holidays there was a mixture of these events: a rock drilling contest, a tug of war between mining crews, speeches, a baseball game, a greased pig event, three legged races, nail driving, mucking contests and even an occasional prize fight were held. One undated Copia holiday photo shows some residents in a parade, dressed in clown costumes. Finally, a dinner, music and a dance at either Keller's Dance Hall, or later at the mine's Donley Recreation center.

Based on historical photos, most of the Labor Day celebration activities were held in front of Keller's Dance Hall. There was an empty space between the Dance Hall and Keller's Hotel. The Dance Hall front porch served as a stage for speakers. In one photo, there was a temporary band stand erected between the Keller Hotel and Dance Hall. The late 1930's mine built recreation center was named after an employee named Donley, likely a miner, who died due to an industrial accident. Donley is spelled different ways, in several documents. Currently, the remains of the Donley is a large slab cement foundation where the recreation hall was, about 1,000 feet up the road, on the right, after you cross Pine Creek.

Historical Copia holiday photos show most of the town was present, observing and participating in the Labor Day and Fourth of July games. Just two photos can be found specifically identifying a

Fourth of July party in Copia. There are many unlabeled celebration photos. Some are labeled Labor Day. Folks were dressed up, men in ties and women in fancy dresses. Surely the saloons did a booming business during the celebrations. No doubt, moonshine from local distillers was discreetly consumed. There was no law enforcement present in the village, except a volunteer sheriff on some Saturday nights.

There is much history presented in Cornucopia photos. Yet, it is very difficult to present a sequential history of the town of before the 1930's. The few records that exist are sporadic. It would have been very helpful if Copia had been incorporated as a town, had a town hall, or even a newspaper. Such was not to be. Let's leave the celebrations, and travel back in time to the beginning of the town of Cornucopia.

---

[1] *A Pictorial History of Gold Mining in the Blue Mountains of Eastern Oregon*, Howard Brooks, Baker County Historical Society 2007, page 157.

[2] https://nepis.epa.gov/Exe/ZyNET.exe/9100P5YI.TXT?ZyActionD.

CHAPTER 2

BIRTH OF COPIA

"Just like a pioneer, in the new frontier, I don't know where to begin...."

"Jupiter Hollow" copyright by The Band, 1969

WOVEN THROUGHOUT COPIA'S HISTORY IS THE MOTIF: WILL the town survive? The same motif applied to the mine. Will Cornucopia continue to be a town, or become a ghost town? Will the mine close and the town wither away? Will heavy winter snows, or summer forest fires destroy the town? Snow and fire could be viewed as dual yin – yang reflections of our own hot and cold human nature. Surely the citizens of Copia were aware of the fate of earlier Oregon gold mining boom towns such as Auburn and later, Greenhorn Oregon. Both towns, when Cornucopia was thriving, had withered to nearly no citizens and ghost town status. They also would have been aware of nearly the entire mining town of Sumter, and then the town of Copperfield burning down. Miners and their families usually moved to new boom towns when their mines closed and jobs ended.

One questionable document gives the first date of miners filing claims in upper Pine Creek Valley, including the Union-Companion above Copia, as 1874, with a boom following in 1875. Wikipedia indicates that Copia was platted in 1886. On the Wikipedia date, at the earlier, downstream, site of Cornucopia (Allentown) buildings were still being moved to the current town site. One 1910 photo of the earlier town site of Allentown, south about one mile from Copia, shows three buildings still remaining. By 1910, most of the Allentown buildings had been moved, or torn down and the materials moved north to Copia.

A website called "Western Mining History" states that gold was discovered in 1880 and in an 1884 dated photo, presented on their website, the town of Copia was already started. So, we have a range of dates from 1880 to 1886 for the start of the town called Copia.

A Western Mining History photo, from the Baker County Library archives, shows a street scene in Copia, labeled 1884. In the photo, there are about 16 buildings in the town, looking down Main Street toward the yet to be built Keller Hotel. It's likely that the photo was dated earlier than it was actually taken. Another possibility is that in 1884 Allentown was still the larger village, while Copia was being built up.

This earlier town site now has only two foundations, concealed by trees and forest duff. Galen West was given land owner (USFS) permission to save, by moving and preserving one of the last small structures from Allentown up to Cornucopia. He was later thwarted by a new and different Forest Service Supervisor, the permission was rescinded. The building later fell down and is now part of the forest duff. The first town site, like Copia, sits near to Pine Creek. Many buildings, including the jail, were moved up the valley from the older Allen Town site, to the current site, around 1885.

Three online history sources, and Pine Valley Museum president Dale Taylor, give a start date of Copia town as 1885. Most of Copia's development occurred from 1885 to the early 1900's. We have a kind of consensus of 1885 as the start date of the town at its current site. The first mayor was Walt Robertson, the second mayor was Nick De Boli. Beyond that, we have no records of the names of Copia mayors until Chris Schneider's statement that he was the mayor in the 1930's.

One could look at Copia as a somewhat ideal small town. Electricity to homes, starting in the1920's, was low cost. Water, provided by a mine built water system, was free. The Cornucopia Mines Company could have charged the mining families whatever they wanted for providing these utilities, but opted for nearly free utilities. At least in the mid-1930's, to early 1940's there was no crime at Copia, according to resident Betty Willette. There will be more of her story later.

Property taxes were very low. According to Baker County

Property Tax offices, even today one of the small gold miner houses and lot is taxed at an average yearly rate of from $300 to $400. The tax office did not have figures going back to the 1920's. An anecdotal tale is that in the 1920's individual houses were taxed at less than 10% of the current tax figure. In the 1920's, perhaps a total of $30. per year was assessed for miner cabin property taxes.

The mine and the town are parts of each other. Cornucopia Mines went bankrupt in 1895, 1904, 1908, 1925 and finally in 1957. During the first four mine company bankruptcies the town lost most of its population. The U.S. Census total in 1930 stated that ten people were living in Copia. This was in stark contrast to when the mine, according to an unverifiable source, employed 700 workers in the early 1900's. By the mid 1950's, only Chris and Jesse Schneider were living in Copia year-round.

The first two commercial structures in Copia were a miner boarding house and a store, both gone. Several structures in Copia burned over the years. The largest store in town, a two story structure called "Cornucopia Trading Company," and later called "Brown and Pierce Store," on the east side of Main Street, burned down in the early 1930's. There is just one mention in the *Pine Valley Echoes* of a fire department in Copia. A fire department was surely needed in a hastily built town of close together wooden buildings heated by wood stoves. Copia was a fire trap of a town with no masonry buildings, except the mine's cement treasury and the powder magazine. Luckily, there were no major fires, nor forest fires that easily could have wiped out the town.

Cornucopia at its peak consisted of: homes and cabins, two hotels (each containing a saloon), five additional saloons, post office, two butcher shops, two general stores, bakery, candy store, post office, school, church, barber shop, two livery stables, at least one hotel and one house where one could purchase personal services from sporting women, a blacksmith and general repair shop, barber shop, community meeting and dance hall, a small sawmill nearby, two miner boarding houses, and the oldest building, the jail.

State of Oregon Department of Geology and Minerals website states:

"The Copia jail was built in Allentown (1885) to meet the community's need to establish and maintain general law-and-order, and then was later moved to the Cornucopia town site in 1889 as mining activity moved upslope closer to the most productive mines. While Cornucopia was not as notoriously lawless as many other frontier communities, the jailhouse were an important institution that fostered stability in a town with numerous saloons and bordellos, and served as a temporary holding place for disorderly citizens...."

CHAPTER 3

1915 Visit, Local and National Politics, Copia Later

"I want to live, I want to give, I've been a miner for a heart of gold"

"Heart of Gold" by Neil Young, copyright Reprise Records, 1971

TO MINE CORNUCOPIA HISTORY, WE RELY ON HISTORICAL photos, historical records, and the tales of citizens to re-create the town. General information about Oregon gold miners can give us an idea of what life was like in the early days of Cornucopia.

Oregon gold miners earned, in 1900, about $4.00 a day. In 2017 dollars, this meant a wage of about $90.00 a day, for between a 10 to 12 hour work day, often seven days a week until about 1915. Around that date, the six day work week came into being at the larger Oregon gold mines.

An online document, dated 1900, no author, states the following costs at non-specified locations in Copia:

All you can eat meal	25 cents
Coffee, bulk beans	15 cents a pound
Mutton (local)	7 cents a pound
Potatoes (likely Eastern OR)	$1.00 per sack (weight unknown)
2 loaves of bread	5 cents

In 1890, a stage coach ride from Baker City to the gold mining town of Cracker (now known as Bourne) cost $3.50 for one person, a distance of about 35 miles. Baggage fees varied from .25 cents for a suitcase to $2.50 for some unknown items. The handwriting of the stagecoach driver is not totally legible. These figures are from a stage coach waybill in the author's collection.

The distance from Copia to Baker City was nearly 62 miles. There were two stage coaches that departed from Copia each day, one to Baker City and one to the nearby town called Union. Based on the stage coach waybill, a fee for a ride from Baker City to Copia would be about $6.50 per person, plus baggage. At the time, this one-way fare, taking two or three days, would cost the equivalent of two or three day's wages for a skilled gold miner. The stage had to cross creeks, bridges were scarce. One source states that it took two days to travel from Baker City to Cornucopia by stage, increasing travel costs by adding food and lodging. There is a mostly original Cornucopia stage coach on display in the Baker City Museum.

The earliest Cornucopia Mines pay records in the large U. of O. Copia archives are from 1919, a $630 monthly wage paid to the then manager, and later primary stock owner of the mine, Robert Betts. The same year, checks were sent to the "Robinette Food Co." for Union Mine boarding house kitchen costs. Many early bills were paid for cord wood, averaging $6.50 to $10 per cord. A good guess is that the different rate depended on the amount of wood purchased. Copia business leader Charles Keller was one of the vendors selling cord wood to the mine. It's doubtful that the owner of several Copia businesses cut the wood himself. The mine bought flour from local "Carson Flour Mills, and (location unknown) Victory Flour Mill."

Copia served as a retail center for the miners and families working for the Red Jacket, Simmons, Norway, Queen of the West and other distant local gold mines up Pine Creek, west and north of town. Teamsters stopping over after delivering goods would have eaten and perhaps stayed overnight in Copia. The town would also have been a place to buy supplies for cattle drovers, sheepherders, loggers, and sales people bringing goods, passing through.

According to Florence Thompson in *Pine Valley Echoes*: "My father used to haul meat to Cornucopia….(from Halfway)….usually by the quarters….to sell to the stores and residents who wintered there….he would tell us about cougars coming down the mountains screaming....behind him, the only way he felt safe was to stop and throw a chunk of meat [to the cougars]."

Many historical photos exist of Copia from 1913 to 1916, taken mainly by Larry Panter. Panter came from Germany, using German cameras. Panter worked for the mine, and later farmed strawberries at Copia. Late in 1915, a boom period started for Copia. 1915 is a good year to look at real and imaginary details of Copia.

Why describe a 1915 visit? Most of the Panter Cornucopia photos are from 1913-1916. 1915 was a microcosm of the history of the town. The year started out with the mine and the town in bust cycle and ended as a booming year for the town. A Baker newspaper business story recorded a big new gold strike near Copia, November 1915. The exact location is not recorded. Cornucopia Mines had been sold in early 1915. One newspaper story listed the price as 'fire sale' low.

A recently posted (online) 1915 article, May 29th, in *The Engineering and Mining Journal* states: "Paul Gaebelein has been made superintendent of the new Baker (gold ore) Mill in Cornucopia." Now we know when the now vanished Baker Mill at Copia started up. Also in 1915, the long Last Chance mine tram was built. The village was thriving, once again.

At the time, liquor and prostitution were big problems in the nearby and bawdy mining town of Copperfield. Copperfield was, as the crow flies, twenty miles from Copia. Cornucopians must have appreciated that State of Oregon law enforcement was focused on Copperfield, and then Cove, allowing them some slack, so to speak. Starting in 1913-1914, continued national bad press labeled Copperfield as "Gomorrah on the Snake River." In 1914, Governor Oswald West sent in his most trusted staffer, the intrepid lawyer Fern Hobbs to clean up Copperfield. She was a powerful, diminutive 26 year old woman. Fern had five state troopers and a prison official for security help.

Upon arrival, Ms. Hobbs ordered the bars and cathouses all closed. When the corrupt mayor and city council ignored her, she revealed an order from the governor declaring martial law. Twenty more National Guard Troops were then sent to make sure the illegal saloons, cathouses, gambling dens and moonshine stills remained shut. Cornucopians also noticed when most of Copperfield, later, burned down. There is now nothing left of Copperfield. Union

County, adjacent to Baker County, had voted to go "dry" in 1914.

The town of Cove, in Union County, was still allowing saloons to serve liquor, despite the county dry law. Cove is about 35 miles, as the crow flies, from Copia. Fern Hobbs was sent to clean up Cove, and she did. Cornucopians were surely relieved that Fern Hobbs did not come to their town, in between Copperfield and Cove. There was a recent television special about the intrepid Fern Hobbs on Oregon's PBS station.

We don't know when prohibition actually started to be occasionally enforced at Copia, perhaps in 1916. That decision would have been a legal, social, political and perhaps budgetary decision by law enforcement and the saloon owners. In addition to the corruption in Copperfield and Cove, some Portland saloon owners paid law enforcement officers not to enforce prohibition. No anecdotes exist of these liquor bribery practices, even political chicaneries, about Cornucopia.

North of Copia, the Lostine River Canyon was widely called "Copper Coil Trail" due to all the bootleg stills operating in the canyon. The efforts of bootleggers operating south of Copia, mostly around Richland, were also under the radar of law enforcement.

Politicians visited Copia once in a while, even in the early days. Oregon Governor Moody visited the town in 1886. One way to accurately examine the political mood of the citizens of Copia in 1915 is to look at election results in Baker County, and political trends at the time in Eastern Oregon. We have no voting records specific to Cornucopia by which to precisely discern the political feelings of the citizens.

We have Baker County voting records to reflect what Cornucopians likely believed. Political trends and national news would have been discussed by Cornucopians. By 1915, Oregonians had been voting directly to elect their senators. In the early 1900's, Oregon's U.S. Senators (as all other states) were all selected by members of state legislature, not by a vote of the people.

The official U.S. Senate webpage states that by 1912 the growing trend amongst states for popular voting to select U.S. senators was called: "The Oregon System." Republicans Fred Mulkey and Jonathan Bourne were the first two Oregon Senators directly elected by a vote of the people; although at the time the state legislature had to ratify the candidate victories first. This was a formality that later was dropped.

Here's a Copia connection. Senator Bourne was a local mining and farming investor. The gold mining town, now ghost town named after Bourne was not too far from Cornucopia. A ghost story is told, later, about a mine near Bourne. The senator invested heavily in mines around Bourne. Surely Senator Bourne would have been discussed by the citizens of Copia. No record exists of Bourne making a campaign visit to Cornucopia, although that is likely. Now, we go to the national political stage, to further examine Baker County voting trends that pertain to Cornucopia.

The last presidential election before our 1915 visit to Copia was the 1912 contest. In the 1912 general election, women could vote for the first time in Oregon. This was well before they were given the vote nationwide in 1920. So, the women of Cornucopia must have had lively political discussions about their first vote. For the 1912 presidential race, Progressive Teddy Roosevelt was nearly as popular, throughout the nation, as Democratic candidate Woodrow Wilson. Both Democratic and Progressive parties and candidates shared many beliefs in 1912. The Progressives championed: nation-wide women's right to vote, some control of big corporations, national direct election of senators, strengthening the 1906 pure food and drug laws, anti-child labor, establishing worker's compensation for injured workers and other issues. Many Progressives also championed nationwide prohibition of liquor, although that issue was not in the Progressive 'platform'.

It's true that a simple vote count does not delve too deep into the mindset of the voter. Yet, we know the Baker County presidential 1912 election 3rd place was held by the incumbent Republican President William Taft. The renegade Progressive Roosevelt, with his metaphoric big stick, beat President Taft and candidate Wilson like gongs in Baker County. In Oregon and in the nation, T.R. would have easily defeated Wilson had the Progressives and the Republicans not split their segment of the vote. Teddy's Cornucopia connections follow.

Teddy Roosevelt, also known as "TR," was the first, if not the only, Vice President to ever tour underground gold mines. This first tour occurred at Colorado's richest gold mine, the Portland, (later combined with the Cresson Mine). Another time, Teddy went into a gold mine in Colorado, also as VP, with President "gold standard" (main campaign issue and motto) McKinley. Both the President and the Vice President touring a dangerous underground mine, together. What would the Secret Service have to say about that, now?

We can infer, due to Roosevelt's big victory in both the 1904 and 1912 Baker County election totals that gold mine visiting TR and his progressive beliefs would likely have been well regarded by the gold miners at Cornucopia. Many Roosevelt campaign buttons, like McKinley's, were colored gold. Roosevelt was also known as an equal supporter of both laborers and management. His slogan for the 1904 election was "A Square Deal" – referring to both labor and management rights. There is a Teddy Roosevelt political cartoon button showing a TR standing between a laborer and a manager, having them shake hands, with the slogan "Justice to All" at the bottom. Of course, TR was also known for many other beliefs, some very controversial. For example, his views about Native Americans would be considered hideous, today.

What this Roosevelt campaign button image brings to mind are generally positive relations, over the years, between Cornucopia managers and laborers, documented in many places in archives. As we know, this was not usually the case in many gold, or especially coal mines.

TR had a strong influence with the development of federal laws governing the use of the lands around Cornucopia. When Cornucopia town started in 1885, there were no National Forests. At the time, there was virtually no federal control over what one did; logging, mining or grazing on forest land. One did have to file a claim to occupy, not just use, vacant unowned land. Land previously utilized by Native Americans. Miners were required to legally register and later own a mining claim. When one invested a certain amount of money, one could "patent" – or keep in perpetuity as long as taxes were paid - a mining claim. The patenting occurred at the county land office in Baker City. National laws had, as now, local effects.

TR's actions affected the Wallowas in many ways. In 1905 Roosevelt created, by decree, the Wallowa National Forest, including the immediate area surrounding Copia and its mines. There was a vast, previously undefined expanse of forest surrounding the village. Also by presidential decree, TR gave the United States Forest Service jurisdiction over the National Forests in 1907, including the Wallowas. Without his, and USFS actions, the meadows and forests of the Wallowas would be "much the worse for wear" than they are now. Especially if there had been unlimited sheep grazing over a long period of time.

In 1915, there still would have been little federal control felt at Copia by citizens. USFS was understaffed, even at the time. The people in Copia, reflected by the Baker County 1916 voting records, still liked TR's progressive beliefs. Despite the beginnings of federal control over much of the forest land; logging, mining and grazing continued with permits.

For the presidential election of 1916, moderate-to-progressive Republican candidate Charles Hughes ran with Teddy's 1904 former Vice President Charles Fairbanks as his VP candidate. They won Baker County by 20%, winning Oregon, too. TR's Progressive Bullmoose party was not active by the 1916 election. Most of the former Bullmoose Progressives backed the Hughes ticket, although some did move to support incumbent Wilson. The 1916 Hughes-Fairbanks Baker County victory also tells us something about the values of the citizens of Copia in 1915.

Hughes lost, by an extremely thin margin, the 1916 national election to incumbent Wilson. The last bearded major party candidate, Hughes, came within a whisker of being elected president. Hughes went on to become Secretary of State, then Chief Justice of the Supreme Court. Later, Hughes was the presiding justice swearing in TR's nephew-by-marriage Franklin Roosevelt at FDR's first inaugural. After that, Baker County voted in four elections to support Democrat FDR. Some said that the veteran public servant Charles Hughes, with his full white beard and deep dish dignity, looked like a stereotyped image of God.

Our tale now returns to 1915 Cornucopia. The first car had traveled the nearby Oregon Trail just ten years earlier. Panter's historical photos show us a town looking like a classic old west mining town with horses and some autos on Main Street. World War One was raging in Europe in 1915. The U.S. and Baker County was seeing a marked shift from horse to automobiles – with horsepower as a numerical strength of these new engines.

There were two stables in town at the time. One bad road went up to Copia, on the west side of Pine Creek. The depression era federally funded new road into town was built later on the east side of Pine Creek. The few automobiles in 1915 Copia were likely not run at night. The old road into town from Halfway was not suited for nighttime travel by automobiles.

Around 1915, Copia had the most saloons in its history. A bachelor miner might deeply miss his family and spend evenings seeking fellowship, drinking beer in the saloons, in an effort to combat loneliness. Cornucopia has no bank in town. Saloons and stores served mining towns as banks. Paychecks were cashed, credit was sometimes given.

A Panter panoramic photo shows the south half of Copia, taken from far up the mountain. 38 structures are in the photo, mostly homes, plus some sheds. Easily identifiable is the Keller Hotel and dance hall to the north of the hotel. This photo allows us to place where some of the businesses of Copia, now gone, were located. Just the back sides of the businesses on the east side of Main Street are visible in the panorama. It's hard to make out which businesses are which on the east side of Main Street, from this looking-westward view. Except, we can see the distinctive sloping roof porch on the north side of the west facing Brown and Pierce general store, clearly visible in the distant panorama.

1915 Cornucopia photos show one and two story wood frame businesses with false fronts. This architecture gave the illusion that the building was larger. Photos indicate very poor street maintenance. The streets were dirt, sloped, with gullies, with an occasional stump smack dab in the middle of the street.

Baseball was popular in Copia, based on the photos of the holiday games on the meadow that later contained the Slum Dam. In 1915, Babe Ruth hit his very first home run as a rookie pitcher for that year's World Champions Boston Red Sox. The Babe went on to hit four home runs during 1915. This was unusual for a pitcher, especially in the dead ball era of baseball. Sports minded Copians probably noticed mentions of the Babe in World Series articles in Oregon sporting pages.

Fourth of July, and other baseball games occurred at Cornucopia in 1915. We have no specific years except one dated photo. Another baseball photo exists of the game being played during the early days. The only flat sports area near the town was right where the Slum Dam was later created.

In 1915 the Ducks and the Beavers played their 18th annual Civil War football game. The Civil War football games started in 1894.

For that time period, there were three years where there was no Civil War game. Two tie games occurred. There were two Civil War games during 1896. Overall, the Ducks thumped the Beavers. The Ducks won thirteen games. The Beavers won three. The Beavers scored zero by the end of most of those games. What fine Duck defensive playing. Cornucopians were surely were aware of the football rivalry by reading Baker and Boise sports pages.

A pathetic entertainment statistic was recorded in 1915. The movie with the highest attendance in the nation was the racist KKK based "Birth of a Nation." Oregon still had many anti-minority laws on the books in 1915. The Klan, in Oregon as well as nationwide, had a viscous and violent disregard for: African-Americans, Jews, Catholics, immigrants in general, and, oddly enough, liquor. The Klan was very active in La Grande. One of the Klan members kept meticulous notes about the secretive La Grande chapter; the records were recently made available for study.

In 1915 Oregon, the Women's Christian Temperance Union and the Anti-Saloon League were gaining popularity. Prohibition did not come to Oregon until 1916. Cornucopia's saloons would have been especially lively on Saturday nights in 1915. Efforts were being made throughout Oregon to pass prohibition laws. Prohibition went into law in Canada in 1915, so miners moving from the goldfields of Canada would have been happy about the easy availability of beer at Cornucopia. By that time, the Yukon gold rush was waning. In general, prohibition was very loosely enforced in Canada. Much whiskey entered the U.S. from Canada.

Like Oregon, the state of Washington banned liquor sales in 1916. A major difference between the states is that Washington allowed individual permits to legally possess a certain amount of alcohol, beyond prescription and religious alcohol. In Spokane County, for example, 34,000 permits were issued for a county having just 44,000 registered voters. Later, the Cornucopia Mines corporate office was based in Spokane.

Oregon's "dry" law of 1916 allowed citizens to possess liquor legally and to bring into the state two quarts of spirits or wine, and six gallons of beer per *month*. In 1921, under federal law, this permission was denied.

With this historical context, now put yourself in the village. It is a fine Cornucopia 1915 Saturday night. You are standing in the dirt street, looking at the front of the three stories Keller Hotel. This is the largest structure in town, if you don't count the Baker mine mill about ¾'s of mile north of Copia. The Lincoln Hotel is close to the left, south of the Keller. The first thing one would notice is the near darkness in the town. Most of the businesses in town had limited electrical power. No street lights were present.

Keller's Hotel had a three story porch all across the front. It was clearly a popular gathering place. The porch was at least thirty five feet long and about seven feet wide. One photo shows about twenty people loitering on the lower porch and steps, plus more hanging out on the second story porch. Other photos also show people lounging on the first and second floor hotel porches. No one is appearing on the Keller third floor porch in any of the photos. Perhaps this was because that floor was the location of the bordello. From the street, one would hear what the people on the lower porch were saying; perhaps you would want to join in the conversation.

To the right of the Keller Hotel was the open area where town folk erected a stage and held Labor Day and some Fourth of July celebrations. North of the hotel stood the Keller Dance Hall. The dance hall was near the site of the 1930's miner's boarding house, currently still standing. Behind you, across Main Street, were stores and two of the town's saloons. Two of the saloons, not sure which ones, were operated by Frank Gallagher.

A 1913 Panter panorama photo shows that the forests around the town had been logged clear cut, more than 100 yards up the mountain in each direction. The area beyond the clearing sur-rounding the town was a vast dark green forest. Cornucopia homes and businesses were wood heated, thus the clearing around the town. Wood cutting also created a safe fire break for the village. There would have been visible kerosene lights in the miners' houses and cabins in and near the town. Due to the general darkness, the miner cabin lights would be shining out of windows like lanterns on distant ships at sea.

Looking from the street inside Keller Hotel at night, there would have been electric lighting in the bar, pool room, restaurant and hotel lobby. It is unlikely that the hotel rooms had electric lighting at the time, just kerosene lamps. Electricity has just been made available to some businesses. Inside the hotel, from the street view, you could see people relaxing, eating, drinking, playing poker and pool. Nothing bright outside was seen except the moon during night time in Copia.

In 1915 the mine had recently set up the primitive electrical grid for the businesses in the town. The power plant was on Pine Creek. Up the mountain, the Union-Companion Mine (Cornucopia Mines owned) had a large on-site steam boiler that generated electricity for the mine and the mill. It is doubtful that one could hear any of the din from Union Mine Mill, two forested miles up hill from town. Cornucopia Mines would build a second hydroelectric power plant, just for the mine, also on Pine Creek, in the early 1920's.

Evening in Copia, one could hear distant noise from the nearest mine mill machinery, the loud Baker Mill ore crusher. Stamp mills make a loud monotonous, rhythmic thumping. That is, if the Baker was running two shifts. The Baker Mill was less than a mile up the canyon, at a similar elevation as the town. Very few records have surfaced from Baker Mill, just anecdotes and photos.

In 1915, the new Baker gold processing mill was not yet owned by Cornucopia Mines. The Baker Mill mainly ran ore from the Last Chance Mine, and other mines in the upper Pine Creek area, such as Queen of the West Mine. Last Chance Mine and Baker Mill were later bought by Cornucopia Mines. Last Chance and Queen of the West ore for the Baker Mill ore was brought down the steep mountain side by tramway. The Tram looked like a ski lift with big buckets. Ore was then hauled from the end of the tram, by wagons and trucks, to the mill.

One can still see tramway cables on the ground up Pine Creek about two miles north of Copia. Several photos of Baker Mill exist on the Baker County Library historical website, three are labeled as such. If a historic photo has the caption "Cornucopia Mill" and it sits near the bottom of the valley, this means the photo is of Baker Mill.

In Copia, in the distance, one would have heard the Pelton water wheels roaring at the town power plant on Pine Creek. Pine Creek itself can make a turbulent roar, too, depending on the level of snowmelt. If the town was in a quite phase, you would hear the rustling of Aspen trees, down by Pine Creek.

Other Copia town evening noises would have been: occasional dog howling – perhaps in response to the yip and yap of coyotes, the yowl of cats, people talking, doors shutting, horses kicking their stalls and neighing in the stables, especially if they hadn't been fed. Another sound might have been the braying mules, or the tinkle of the mule's belles. That is, if the freighters spent the night in Copia and had left their mules, still harnessed, in the stable's corral. Mining mules wore bells. This mythical visit to the town is in summertime, when there were many more horses in town than in wintertime. The sound of kindling and firewood being split for cooking was likely to be heard. Wood cutting was a never ending task for homes and businesses.

Dishes and glasses would have been clinking, washed and stored in the restaurant and saloon kitchens. The shuffling of chairs on wooden floors, perhaps an owl could be heard hooting in the close-by forest. Noises of occasional arguments and laughter in the saloons would be clear. On weekends, you would hear bar and/or dance hall music consisting of: a violin, banjo, accordion, drum, guitar, piano or trumpet. We now call this music 'Americana'.

On this summer 1915 Saturday night, there surely was a small, local band playing in the Keller Dance Hall, followed by applause. Come on in, have a beer and enjoy the fun. Later, the band would have been the Schneider Family Band playing with Chris Schneider playing lead on fiddle. You would hear the sound of children playing in the miners' cabins. Some cabins were near the center of the town.

One would smell: wood smoke from stoves, pine trees, the dust and dirt of the unpaved streets, cooking from the restaurants and cabins, tobacco smoke, perhaps a whiff of outhouses, street horse dung and the smell of ever popular beer from the saloons. According to miner Dale Holcomb, the saloon beer was generally pumped from a keg into small, tin, individual drinking buckets. "Last living Copia miner" Dale Holcomb, sadly now gone, still had his Copia saloon beer drinking bucket in his possession.

The grocery stores would smell of local produce, crated inside. The stores surely had dust and musty odor problems, due to the street dirt drifting inside. Dominique Soldini's meat market would have strongly smelled like beef, lamb, turkey, and or chicken. Surely Soldini's family emigrated from Italy, at some time in the past. The large livery stable across the street would have had a pungent barnyard odor. Later, the Motley family bought the meat market, owning it for many years.

Consider, except on Saturday nights, a relatively peaceful town. On weekends, it was a rambunctious gold mining town, but not a rowdy as one would think. You might hear an occasional fight at the dance hall or a bar on weekend nights. According to gold miner Dale

Holcomb's stories, the fights were often between miners and cowboys.

We know there was lots of beer, some wine and moonshine drinking in Copia. Wine would have been expensive. Keller Hotel served alcohol as did the next door Lincoln Hotel. Across the street from Keller's were the Gallagher and Curran Saloon, and the Cornucopia Saloon. Charley Keller's saloon "Miner's Resort" used to be between the Keller Hotel and the Keller Dance Hall. A 1915 Main Street photo primarily shows the Keller Hotel. In the photo, Keller's Miner's Resort Saloon, next door to the hotel in the photo, was lying in ruins. The Miner's Resort was probably flattened by snow. At least two other names-not-known saloons served gold miners for many years. In addition to the four saloons and two hotels, the nearby Keller Dance Hall sold beer.

An undated saloon token (coin) has the wording "Keller's Saloon-Richland" on one side, and "good for one smile" on the other side. Western saloon tokens often state "good for one beer." The location of Keller's first saloon was in nearby Richland. This was Charley Keller's only known pre-Copia business.

Charley Keller operated four known businesses in Copia, and earlier one in Richland, selling liquor, amongst his other business interests. When one puts two and two together, it has a predictable outcome. For Keller, bootleggers were known to operate nearby in Richland (and in the Snake River and Lostine Canyons). Not saying that Keller was a bootlegger. But, he was a smart businessman who would have benefitted by buying and selling the cheaper tax-free moonshine, along with other liquor, in his businesses.

Keller had compelling reasons not to have it known that he possibly trafficked in 'tangle leg' illicit whiskey. He had to obtain state and federal liquor licenses that could be revoked. He surely didn't want any of his businesses shut down due to problems with officials.

Cornucopians involved with the liquor business must have known prohibition was coming to Oregon, based on gossip and newspaper articles. In Portland, some saloon keepers simply took their business sign down and put up one saying "Pharmacy." This was a bit of a nationwide trend when prohibition became law nationwide. A pharmacy (saloon) patron had to show a doctor's Rx. A record was made of this, and then the customer was served the legal amount of liquor stated on the prescription. This was, depending on the doctor's Rx, up to a pint a day.

Federal prohibition law allowed Catholic and Jewish church and synagogue officials to sell ten to fifteen gallons of sacramental wine or brandy, each year, to each family that were church or synagogue members. The religion of the Keller family is unknown. We don't know if liquor distribution practices, dodging around the law, occurred in Copia, except the often reported use of moonshine whiskey.

The largest non-mine employer in Copia was clearly the Keller family. In addition to the hotel and store, this family of entrepreneurs owned the nearby Keller Dance Hall, and before it fell down, the Keller Saloon. It is unknown how long all four Keller businesses operated. The structures are now gone. The Keller Hotel was on the west side of Main Street. The hotel started out as Jesse Alberson's Hotel. An approximate start date of the hotel would be around 1895-1900. The twice daily stage coaches stopped in front of the town's largest building – The Keller Hotel.

A 1907 photo shows a fairly new looking Keller Hotel with a sign hanging from the porch stating "Cash Store." The store would have been in the hotel building. In addition to the store, inside: hotel office, a bar with pool room, a restaurant and a bordello on the premises. It was like an old west shopping mall, right inside the Keller Hotel. In the photo a stage coach is being loaded to capacity in front of the hotel.

Lambert Florin's book *Ghost Towns of the West* states that at Copia's Keller Hotel the Madame's first name was Fanny. Fanny ruled the third floor cathouse within the hotel. Fanny is such a classic name for a bordello madam.

A tale in *Pine Valley Echoes* states that a brick of solid gold was laid out on the bar at the Keller Hotel. The barkeep, Charley Keller himself in one photo, would give it to anyone who could lift it with one hand. No one could lift it. Hundreds tried, resulting in a highly polished gold brick on the bar. Gold brick molds make a brick that is narrower at the top than at bottom, making it even harder to lift. If the gold brick on the Keller bar weighed, as many gold bricks do, 439 ounces, it would be currently be worth about one half a million dollars at the current value of gold. Close by, the Keller Dance Hall was rented out for community events. Dances at the Keller Dance

Hall are later described in Betty Willete's narrative.

Charley Keller was born in Kentucky.[1] Keller was born during the Civil War and migrated, date unknown, to eastern Oregon. In the late 1880's, Cornucopia Mines was owned by a Kentucky syndicate called "Oregon Gold Mining Company." Could Keller have heard about Copia in Kentucky? His parents, according to the federal Census of 1920, were born in Germany. Chris Schneider's family also came from Germany. Keller married Dora, also born in Germany. In his saloons in Richland and Copia, we could speculate that Keller might have used German brewing techniques to brew beer. It is unknown whether Charley ever brewed his own saloon beer.

In 1915, most of the major breweries in the United States were owned by families originally from Germany. Schlitz, Busch, Schmidt, Hamm, Pabst, and others all had German roots. In Portland, Henry Weinhard, of German heritage, brewed four non-alcoholic beers during prohibition. These were all legal, tax-paying and regulated breweries. The breweries survived prohibition by selling other beverages.

The most popular one was called "Malt Syrup." At home, all one had to do was add yeast, water, and the result was beer. According to a census publication, between 1900 and 1915, more than 6.2 million immigrants from southern and eastern Europe arrived in the U.S. Basque and Italian immigrants would have been part of this number. Germans were counted in a different document.

The bootlegging industry was a good fit for some of these immigrants. This is a business that has no entrenched establishment, little capital required, and demanded no particular training except the knowledge of one semi-skilled bootlegger. The immigrant families often worked together in family owned businesses. There were Basques and Italians living in Cornucopia.

The Keller Hotel and Dance Hall changed hands, but stayed in the family. Charley Keller's daughter, Hazel, married Haymond Swisher. The Keller Hotel then came to be called Swishers. The son-in-law and daughter, the Swishers, took over Charley's businesses in Copia. The Swishers also came from Germany. In addition to the Keller, Schneider, Panter and Swisher families, there were other families of German heritage in early Cornucopia.

Was any German style food offered at Copia's restaurants and saloons? Could the Germans in Copia have climbed Cornucopia Peak wearing leather lederhosen and thick wool knee socks for Bavarian-themed Wallowa Mountains hikes? Wearing those, using an ice ax or an alpenstock, one would be safe, warm and comfortable while hiking. A European architectural alpine theme is currently seen on some of the structures on the south end of Wallowa Lake. Is there a distant echo of "Yo da leh hee hoo" echoing on the steep rocky glacial walls of Pine Valley? Try it. Yodeling is fun, especially with an echo from mountain walls.

The stagecoach ride from Cornucopia to either Halfway or Cove must have been scary at times for passengers. It is known that the early road on the west side of Pine Creek sloped, at times, towards a cliff drop off. The drivers would ask passengers to move to the uphill side of the coach to balance the coach to avoid a wreck over the cliff. A few Oregon history photos show stage coaches on narrow, sloped and perilous mountain roads.

An undated 1900-1910 photo shows the inside of Keller Miner's Resort Saloon, with Charley and a helper behind the bar. Keller sports a handlebar mustache with an ornate Pabst Blue Ribbon advertising sign behind the bar. This is evidence that Charley probably did not brew his own beer in Copia. There are about a dozen bottles on the back bar shelf. It's impossible to tell whether these were whiskey bottles or not.

No records have been found how the rooms were furnished inside the Keller or the next door Lincoln Hotels. Small town hotel rooms, at the time, did not have private bathrooms. There was a large water pitcher and ceramic washbasin on a table or bureau in better quality hotel rooms. The Keller's likely supplied these items in their better quality hotel rooms.

Likely the Keller or the Lincoln hotels created a typical hotel market niche in Copia by offering a few rooms set up to accommodate more affluent visitors. This was a common practice in gold mining towns, as it is in many hotels today. A high-end visitor could be a gold mines stock broker, a mine or mill manager staying for a meeting with Cornucopia Mines management. These customers would be able to pay more for a room. A room containing perhaps pictures on the walls, a rug and fresh daily linens. Thread count for hotel linens, a mini-bar? Forget it.

Galen West tells of roaming inside the abandoned, ramshackle Keller Hotel several times in the 1950's. Don't you wish you could have done that? Galen states there was decrepit and broken furniture strewn about. On the first floor, he could tell where the hotel office and restaurant used to be. It was not evident where the 'cash store' in the hotel used to be. There was a large bar on the north side, with a long glass mirror all along the back wall. On the second floor, the rooms were all the same, not very large. Galen was young at the time, and does not remember what the bath rooms or third floor were like.

Sometime in the mid-to-late 1920's, Charley and Dora Keller left Copia and disappeared. They left, probably, after the mine's bankruptcy of 1925. Seeking any more information about Charley Keller or Dora after Copia, there is nothing to be found. Lots of false leads occurred in the process of my searching for information about the Kellers.

A family named Keller started a Hood River beer brewing supply company in the 1980's. Those Kellers had sold the business. After many calls, I reached an elderly lady named Keller, who used to own the beer supply business in the gorge. She knew nothing about, nor was related to the Kellers of Copia. The Copia Kellers fade into the dim mists of time, like ghosts.

The Swishers, as the Keller's did, rented hotel rooms to any customers: miners, vendors, visitors and government workers. Copia was in a bust cycle, nearly empty by the mid 1920's. There would have been few customers for the Swishers. In the 1930's, the hotel and dance hall were sold to the Smelcer family.

In the 1930's, the new federally funded road to town, on the east side of Pine Creek, was being built by federal employees of Works Project Administration (WPA), and groups of prisoners. This government infrastructure project was mainly created to benefit Cornucopia Mines. The federal employees were all housed in Smelcer's (formerly Keller, then Swisher) Hotel. The original Copia dance hall, in front of which the community celebrations were held, would have been enjoyed by WPA employees until 1939, when the mine funded the construction of the wonderful new Donley recreation center. The Donley building included a maple dance floor.

The only current evidence of Keller's Hotel: some bricks, a mostly buried safe, and a partially filled in three sided field stone cellar. The cellar was built into the mountain about 30 feet west from the existing road. The broken bricks in the forest duff at the site of the hotel's porch have the label "Weiser." Weiser was the name of the brick works nearby in Idaho. The landscape has changed too much to determine the footprint of the hotel or dance hall sites, without owner permission for some excavation.

The space between the hotel and dance hall, where the community celebrations were held, is now densely covered with trees and forest duff. An undated historical photo of Copia shows a Labor Day celebration crowd with a bandstand sitting in the empty space between the hotel and Keller Dance Hall. It's likely that lumber from ruins of Keller's Miner's Resort Saloon were recycled to build the town bandstand on the same site.

Immediately next to the Keller Hotel, to the south, was the Lincoln Hotel. The Lincoln was built with profits from the Simmons gold mine, four miles up Pine Creek from Copia. Clem and Clair Lincoln ran the hotel. A 1920 photo identifies the former Lincoln Hotel as the Tedrowe Hotel. The Lincoln-Tedrowe Hotel site was an empty lot by the 1930's. The Lincoln hotel was torn down, date unknown according to *Pine Valley Echoes* magazine. Could it be that materials from the demolished Lincoln were used to help build the currently existing miner's boarding house?

Heavy snow loads on roofs was a consistent problem for the town. Snow crushed several buildings in Cornucopia. Winter was not just a season in Cornucopia; it was more like an industry. Deep winter snows hold Copia in a silent grip. One had to get up on the roof of the cabin, or business to shovel and saw the snow off at least once each winter. This was difficult with the steep roof pitches. Otherwise, odds were that the heavy snow load would crush the building. Two photos show snow shoveling ladders attached, going up roof pitches. Locals used six foot long crosscut logging saws, one person on each side, to carefully saw through the snow and ice in sections, then push sawed segment off the roof. After all, if one cut into the roof at all while sawing snow, there would be a leak.

Snow sheds were sometimes built between a house and the outhouse, so one could access the outhouse without shoveling snow. The Schneiders did this, the shed between the house and outhouse was still standing until 2010. The long Schneider shed had two parts called dog and cat heaven. These sheds might double as a firewood storage area. Felling, bucking, splitting and stacking enough firewood for the winter was a time consuming task for a mining family.

Each home stockpiled preserved food, in case of winter shortages at the local grocery. Due to deep snow, if the horse-drawn hauling sleds from Halfway could not get up to Copia, locals might have to wait a few days to buy groceries while the grocery store ran low on inventory. If the family had a hunter, or traded with a hunter, there would be dried and salted venison and elk meat in the larder. The favorite preserved or dried fruit were the local strawberries and huckleberries.

A bridge existed over Pine Creek at Copia capable of heavy loads from the early days of the town. Pine Creek itself is an integral part of Copia, flowing through town. The normally placid creek, sometimes in spring and early summer, would become a tumultuous water course. Pine Creek could tear out trees to add to the power of a snow melt flood. A few of the early miner cabins were built too close to the creek, and were washed out. There are stories about a couple of drownings in Pine Creek at Cornucopia.

Pine Creek can sing, it can roar. The music of the creek depends on the season. There were two mine-built power plants on Pine Creek. One was at the south end of the town provided power for the town's needs. Another power plant for the mine was about a mile below the town. Both power plants are now gone. The bogeymen snow and Pine Creek eventually demolished them. The death of Pine Creek occurs when it flows into the Snake River at Hells Canyon Reservoir. Now, taking irrigation water from Pine Creek is strictly regulated and monitored by local and state authorities.

In mining days, with law enforcement rarely ever coming to Copia, people policed themselves. There are many references to bootleg whiskey, called tanglefoot, being available on the sly. Even during prohibition some residents would have had a personal bar of saved, or bootleg, or smuggled whiskies in their homes. Were any of the Cornish gold miners able to afford Scotch whiskey? According to mining historian Miles Potter, Cornucopia passed a city ordinance, date unknown, prohibiting sales of liquor stronger than beer or wine. Did citizens obey their own ordinance? Miles Potter contends that the miners of Copia preferred beer over hard liquor, anyway.

Cornucopia was unlike a typical western-movie gold mining town. No stories exist of fighters or drunks being thrown through the swinging saloon doors into the street. We don't know if there even were swinging saloon doors. No gunfights were recorded. There is record of a 1905 shooting occurring on the road going up to both Union and Mayflower mines. The shooting was over use of the same road by both companies.[2]

No records of smashing of saloon windows, except much later by vandals. On Saturday nights, a temporary unpaid Sheriff was appointed by the citizens of the town. Mostly there was no sheriff at all. No Matt Dillon or Wyatt Earp types existed at Copia.

Perhaps stories will emerge from family histories that would revise our somewhat peaceful image of Copia. On most nights in Copia one would have seen, smelled and heard a small western mining town going about its normal business. A booming gold town business was going on.

Moving forward from our imaginary 1915 visit to the town, the mine financed the building of a large, new, two room schoolhouse in 1916. Unlike the old school, the new school had inside bathrooms. Not much information is available about the town of Copia during the 1920's. We know the mine laid off most of its workforce in 1925. 1925- 1926 was one of the few times that the mine shut down altogether. We know the town nearly drained of residents by the late 1920's.

A nationwide lack of more than token enforcement of prohibition, in the 1920's, surely was noticed in Copia. According the book *Last Call* by Danile Okrent, Detroit had over 20,000 Speakeasies (and other illegal type bars) and New York City had over 30,000 establishments like that. This is such a high figure, that it is difficult to believe.

Random bits of information from the 1920's, courtesy of the U. of O. Knight Library and the Pine Valley Community Museum archives: Farmer Lawrence Panter bought fuse and dynamite from the mine supplies warehouse, likely used to clear stumps for his strawberry farm, the mine lost a lot of money in winter-1922, about $70,000 to $80,000 per month (figure could be skewed if the mine was only doing 'development' during those months – not mining ore), losses in winter of 1927 varied from $2,000 to $5,000 per month, in 1925 the mine paid $150. burial costs for Dale Taylor's great grandfather, M. Updike. This is the only funeral cost entry found in the ledgers.

The stock market crash in 1929 meant for Baker County that there were few jobs and little money available for business growth or investment. Yet, just as the depression deepened, Cornucopia started another boom cycle. In the early 1930's, Robert Betts invested a lot of his fortune in a new corporate version of the mine. Betts lived the fiscal aphorism – "sell when high, buy when low." Well-paying mine jobs, with medical benefits that were then available, even during the depression, in Copia.

If a youth was not suited for a mining or mine mill job in Depression era Copia, there were two 1930's Civilian Conservation Corps camps hiring near Baker City. CCC paid a "dollar a day" wage. This was meant as a starting wage for youth. Part of your paycheck was sent back to one's parents.

"They [the youthful CCC total nationwide workforce] were soon supplemented by some 20,000 local experienced men: lumber jacks, hunting guides and the like." These older CCC workers taught the younger workers how to work in the woods. 25,000 Veterans were hired to also serve as teachers-leaders. 15,000 Native Americans were hired by the CCC, ensuring a diverse workforce.[3]

CCC projects near Copia included building the USFS Two Color Guard Station on Main Eagle Creek, and the USFS Halfway area Ranger Station. CCC workers also received limited medical and dental care, some for the first times in their lives.

Over the years, there were several doctors hired by the Cornucopia Mines to tend to miner and miner families. There are ledger entries for a Halfway dentist having part of his practice paid for by the mine. Earlier, the mine had established one of the first HMO's (Health Maintenance Organization) in Oregon. The gold miners paid a one dollar monthly fee to the mine. They were provided with health care, including hospitalization, if needed, in the Baker City hospital. It's unknown what the miner families paid for their medical care.

In the late 1930's Cornucopia Mines hired a new company doctor, Robert Pollack, M.D. Later, Pollack wrote an autobiographical book about his lifelong medical practice, his experience in World War II, and his trainings, including his experiences in Cornucopia. Parts of Dr. Pollack's book provide a valuable source of information about life in Copia in the 1930's.

Dr. Pollack was a brusque and scrappy individual. His book includes stories of fist fights the Doctor was involved in. Some Copia miners decided that he was too brusque with them. One of the biggest, strongest and meanest miners with two sidekicks confronted

Doctor Pollack outside his clinic at the Copia Mine buildings. They demanded that he treat the miners better, or threatened violence. The Doctor hauled off and kicked the big miner hard, right in his private parts. As the big ruffian was doubled over in pain, the Doctor prescribed an instant knockout punch upside the miner's head. Anesthetic for the pain of the groin kick. The big miner was out cold, crashing to the ground like a logged tree. The other two miners wisely fled the scene.

Dr. Pollack's book provides vivid medical detail about life in the village. The doctor critiques both the mine and the miners of Cornucopia:

> "Adjacent to the mine office.....a well-equipped surgery [his clinic], the Cornucopia segment of the practice was pure socialize[d] medicine....a common expression, used by Cornucopians in reference to their more than liberal morals...'there are three shifts in Cornucopia, one coming in the front door, one in bed, and one leaving the back door.'"

The doctor is referring to the sometimes brisk business for the cathouses and their customers in town.

Dr. Pollack continues his narrative with a story about a lift operator, inside the mine, who abused the Doctor and a companion with a prank. Pranks were common in Copia. The Doctor was being sent down the main shaft, in an ore skip (a large bucket), to attend to a mine accident victim. When they came to a jolting stop at one of the mine level stations, the companion with the Doctor, inside the mine bucket with him, states to Pollack: "He sure slammed on those frigging [mine lift] brakes. That was for your benefit, Doc. God dammed jailbird." Doctor: "Is the hoist man [operator] a jailbird?" "Doc, the son of a bitch just got out of the state pen."

After release from jail, the employee mentioned must have previously worked as a hoist operator. Large mines like Copia would not risk on-the-job training for this vital position. They hired hoist operators with experience. Smaller, lower paying mines had to train some hoist operators from scratch. Hoist operators filled a position that was critical to mine safety.

The operator had to carefully listen to the number of wire pull operated bell signals indicating what was expected of him. A certain number of pulls indicated just ore on the way up the shaft, or the number of bell pulls that indicated that an emergency had occurred and an injured miner was coming up. The operator, above, at the levers of the hoist engine, could not see down into the shaft to the level, far below, where he was to start, or stop the lift. No in-mine telephone system existed. The operator also relied on a nearby large wheel that gave the location of the station, or level, in the mine shaft, thus the location of the skips (or ore buckets) within the shaft. Safety and miner health were very important to the Cornucopia Mining Company. Mine records validate this necessity. Doctor Pollack commented in his book on an outbreak of V.D. in Copia:

"My first trial with a gonorrhea outbreak which reached epidemic proportions before it was quelled.....a girl arrived at the mining camp and established herself in the upper room above the Basques barber shop."

Later, miners:

"came trooping in droves to my office seeking cures.....the sequel which occurred seemed almost unbelievable. A miner, one of the original victims of the outbreak, married the instigator.....I often wondered what rules he instigated to control his wife's chastity."

This story illustrates part of the boom cycle in the mining town; disposable income for the gold miners.[4] The doctor's comments about the Basque barber and tales about Basque sheepherders are two of the few instances to be found highlighting cultural diversity in Cornucopia.

The Basque language contains eight different dialects. No direct link has been found with any other language and the Basque. These mountain people had their own European nation until the 1500's. Like Cornucopians, Basques are a fiercely independent and hard-working people. An economic part of Copia was the twice yearly presence of sheepherders. The herders were mostly Basque taking their flocks to and from summer pastures up in the Wallowas.

Today, one can eat at an outstanding Basque restaurant south of Copia in Jordan Valley. A Basque Fall Festival livens up the small town yearly. Basque sheepherders still work the high deserts of eastern Oregon. The sheep industry continues despite economic cycles.

When a town's main employer, such as Cornucopia Mines, goes

bankrupt, the town's bust – or borrasca – cycle starts. The people who did not leave Copia immediately upon mine shutdown have to be very resourceful to make their livings. Some went to Halfway during summer and fall to work for the nearby ranches and farms. In winter, moving to Halfway would have been difficult. Farms and ranches did not hire extra hands in winter, anyway.

Government programs were few. Worker's Compensation Insurance did not even start in Oregon until 1914. Before that year, if you lost your arm in a mining accident, you were treated for the injury and then lost your job. Likely, you had to go without any compensation for the lost arm.

Citizens of Cornucopia had to fend for themselves. Their fall back plan would be to move away and seek other jobs if times got too hard in Copia, or they could no longer perform their job. There were State of Oregon unemployment benefits for the miners, started early in Franklin Roosevelt's administration, around 1935. Beyond unemployment insurance, there were no adequate family welfare benefits available to speak of until well after the mine closed.

Despite a boom at Copia, the effects of the depression started to be strongly felt by Baker County citizens by 1932. New federal government welfare, a 1932 President Hoover program called relief, amounted to slightly less than $1.00 a day per family. The family was also given three quarts of milk a week, for an impoverished family of five. Smaller families got less. This limited welfare was for buying food, paying for housing and all other expenses. In 1931, and earlier, there were no governmental welfare or food programs available at all. There was some depression time funding for soup and bread kitchens in big cities.

A five person family, if unable to find any work, would be trying to exist on less than a 1932 dollar a day. That's for all living expenses combined.[5] If they paid rent, they might go hungry, especially if they had no savings. The family of five would be barely able to afford to eat even with the new government help. Churches and soup kitchens provided some additional charity to the poor. The help provided to the poor was so inadequate, that even bootlegger Al Capone started, mainly for public relations reasons, a soup kitchen in Chicago.

Worst case scenario would be for a family to become homeless, living on the edges of a road in a self-made shack. The roadside shacks started appearing in western Oregon in 1930-1931. Groups of these shacks were often called Hoovervilles, named in derision after President Hoover.

To compare the dollar a day family of five welfare income to the average wage of a Cornucopia gold miner, in 1933 the miner pay was about $5.50 a day. In today's dollars this daily mine pay amount would be about $100. The wage was paid for six work days a week, with unpaid Sunday off. Plus, as mentioned, the mine provided nearly free water and power, low rent for decent housing and low fee recreation hall usage, and nearly free health care. The miners, according to several sources, felt very fortunate to have good paying jobs, healthcare and other benefits, during the depression.

No government funded re-training programs existed for Copia's laid off workers. These came much later - early 1970's. The late 1940's World War II Veteran's G.I. Bill was our first national federal re-training act. Cornucopia Mines honored veterans, with an active recruiting and benefit program aimed at World War I veterans. Based on the mine's end of World War I veteran recruiting efforts, it's possible the mine had an earlier recruiting program for Spanish American War veterans, but no documentation is available about that.

Economic diversification is now cited as a panacea for a town which loses its main employer. There was no economic diversification at Copia. There were mainly mining and mining dependent businesses at Copia. Cornucopia Mines, even during bust and bankrupt times, kept at least two or three employees on the payroll, to protect its massive investments: the mine and the mine mill equipment. These jobs were funded for security and maintenance, in case the mine started up again, or the company sold the mine.

The mine ledgers at the U. of O. are all from the 1930's, showing profits and little debt at the time of mine closing in 1941. The Copia Mines ledgers at the Pine Valley Community Museum do have a few fragmentary details from the years 1915 to 1930. Like the records at the U. of O. library, there is no long term sequence of mine records or ledgers. For most years of the operation of the mine, the mine's ledgers are missing.

Family detail about Copia is contained in the miner letters archived at the Pine Valley Community museum. Family letters dwell on the routine issues and challenges that families have: discussing what family members are doing, births and deaths, where non-local relatives are living, and what they are doing. There are two mine payroll ledgers at the Pine Valley Museum, but like the six ledgers at the U. of O., they have no overall end of year profit figures for the entire operation. These figures must be in missing ledgers. The Pine Valley Community Museum has a trove of Copia photos. The Baker County Library also has a trove of Cornucopia photos. These photos are available for viewing on line. Few photos of Cornucopia Mine or town are in the two boxes of Copia records at the U. of O. Library.

A rare photo shows the inside of "Cornucopia General Store-1895-1910." In the store photo, there are canned goods, hardware, clothing, chairs, a couch, and lots of unidentifiable small items for sale. The name of the store is not given.

An undated, early photo, also from Baker County Library, shows a store on the east side of Main Street with the caption "Cornucopia Company Store." Based on the mine ledgers, no groceries were sold by the mine store. Many records exist of credits for purchases such as hardware from the Cornucopia Mines Warehouse, perhaps from this store. At least one privately owned general store featured groceries and items gold mine families would need. The same store labeled earlier as the Cornucopia Company Store was labeled in several other photos as the Brown and Pierce general store.

By the 1930's, the Brown and Pierce store, the largest store in town, had been destroyed by fire. There were smaller grocery and general stores at the time. Limited hardware and clothes were available for purchase on credit in the mid-1930's at the then new company warehouse. The warehouse was near the mine mill. These purchases were only for mine employees.

The company warehouse goods appearing on purchase orders: used and new rainwear (the mine was very wet inside), belts, shoes, safety gear, and even some exotic items such as fishing lures. Documented in the mine ledgers at the U. of O. library, for several of the years of the warehouses existence, the company lost money when the entire year's totals were recorded. This is an indication of an altruistic employer, not an "owe my soul to the company store" (mining song) employer who would always charge very high prices, and always make a profit for goods sold to miners. Goods were expensive in any case, due to the extra expense of hauling goods up to remote Copia.

In 1938, Cornucopia Mines constructed sixteen nearly identical, quality two story homes for employee families on the east side of Pine Creek. The location was not far from the slum dam, south of the current turn off to Cornucopia Lodge. This mine subsidized housing consisted of 24 by 24 foot homes, rented at low cost to mine employees. All the homes had water and electricity. There is nothing left in Copia of these homes, as they were cut in half and sold by the mine for hauling down to Halfway. A few of the 1938 Copia miner homes still exist, after being hauled down to Halfway. As before, Cornucopia today has a mixture of private and mine owned structures.

It was not only Cornucopia Mining Company that was, generally, very good to their employees. Near Ouray, Colorado, the Camp Bird Mine was also known to treat their miners well. The mine owner, Tom Walsh, had earlier been an hotelier. He funded quality, tasty boarding house food for gold miners, on china plates. The rooms in the boarding house had each just two beds, two miners per room. Polished hardwood floors, hot water in the bathrooms, and a free library were all enjoyed by employees. Like Cornucopia, Camp Bird was located deep in a remote forested valley.

Three sawmills supplied lumber for the town of Cornucopia and local mine needs. Some of the mills lumber probably was sold in Halfway. The closest was called The Melhorn Sawmill. One record shows the Melhorn starting in the 1890's. It was located about one mile north of the Copia, where East Pine Creek entered Pine Creek. Nothing remains of the Melhorn, today. Another sawmill, date unknown, was at Frog Lake, about two miles south and east of the town. The third sawmill, perhaps called the Goodwin, was near Mud Lake, south-east of the town.

The oldest business use building still existing in Copia is the two story, leaning, miner boarding house, north of the Keller Hotel site. The building date is unknown, possibly built in the early 1930's. Ann Ingalls states that there was another two story boarding house, now gone, right to the north of the existing, leaning, building. A second story covered walkway, above snow level, went between the boarding houses. The boarding houses were very near, if not at, the site of the Keller Dance Hall.

After the mine closed in 1941, there were only three mine jobs left. In 1942, the federal government made sure any gold and silver mines, like Cornucopia, would not re-open during WW II. The government created the "Limitation Order # 208 of the War Production Board." Mines with war needed minerals continued to operate. Copia town went bust again. Cornucopia village was quiet for many years.

The Cornucopia pack station was opened by Eldon Deardorf of Richland in the early 1960's. A few people work at the Copia pack station, which is, still, open from summer to fall. The end of the funding for Chris Schneider's fulltime caretaker job at the mine occurred in the mid 1950's. In 1980-'81 there were fulltime jobs created in Cornucopia by United Nuclear Company. Except the UNC miner jobs, the town had no year-round jobs available for decades.

Around 1945, four years after the mine closed all of Copia's stores and businesses had closed as well. The Keller Hotel was still standing, as was the candy store, the town's power house on Pine Creek and several other civic buildings. In the mid-1970's heavy snow load finally took those structures. Blair Sneddon states that the last business open in town was either Gorman's Grocery Store with a gas pump in front of the store, or the Peterson Grocery Store. These two businesses were on the south end of town, near the Schneider home. Nothing remains of the last two mining-era retail businesses.

In the late 1970's, preparation for mining by United Nuclear Co. started. Business in the Copia area was sporadic, with seasonal logging. Cornucopia was truly a ghost town during winter each year beginning in the 1960's when the elderly Schneiders, the last family living in Copia year-round, moved from Copia to Halfway. That's over thirty years of winter full-time ghost town status for Copia.

In Copia, United Nuclear Company started a new shaft to connect to an inner part the collapsed Colter Adit, and started re-timbering the Colter Adit in 1981. These efforts stopped in 1982. No gold was mined in Copia, just preparation for mining.

All right, dear reader, it's time to fess up. If you have the antique glass-bulb tall gas hand pump from Copia's main street in front of Swisher's Cornucopia Store, no matter how you got it, please donate it to the Pine Valley Community Museum. This act of kindness will erase a stain on your soul or karma. If you have the faded sign that says "Keller Hotel and Bar," you have to donate it, too. Do it, if only for the tax deduction.

[1] *Hells Canyon Journal*, Sybyl Smith, June 10th 1992 page 11.
[2] 1981 *Pine Valley Echoes*, page 16.
[3] *Traitor To His Class*, H.W. Brands, Doubleday Printers, New York, 2008, pages 30-31.
[4] *The Education of a Country Doctor*, Robert Pollack, M.D. by Vantage Press 1978, pages 63, 65, 69 and 125.
[5] *The Autobiography of William O. Douglas (Supreme Court Justice)*. Delta Books, Dell Publishing, New York, 1974, page 354.

CHAPTER 4
POPULATION, EMPLOYMENT, STATE HELP

"Now I am back in the Mountains
With my pick and my shovel in my hand"

"Californy Gold" by Woody Guthrie, public domain

AN EXACT WAY TO LOOK AT THE HISTORY OF COPIA IS TO look at the U.S. census and state of Oregon records. Below is a table giving the public record of the number of people living in Copia every ten years, and some data on mine employment. The census data tells a tale of a town nearly dying in the 1920's, and then coming back to life in the 1930's. There is no census data available from before 1900. Recently released State of Oregon Archives also helps us look at the town accurately.

Online U.S. Census Data for Cornucopia documents a never incorporated town. The number of people working for Cornucopia Mines in 1885, according to Wikipedia, is "approximately 350." One source states that the mines peak employment year was 1915, with no backup documentation. Other sources offer very different peak employment figures, such as "over 700 employees," dates unknown.

As the workforce at the mine grew, the number of businesses and people in Cornucopia also increased.

Year	Copia's Town Population	Cornucopia Mines # of Employee Estimates
1880's-90's	Unknown	700 (Carter's *Ghost Towns of the West*)
1885	500 (Wikipedia)	Unknown
1900	332 (U.S. Census)	176 (Brooks' *Pictorial History of Gold*)
1910	132 (U.S. Census)	105 (letter, U. of O. Knight Library records)
1920	242 (U.S. Census)	130 (document, U. of O. Knight Library records)
1930	10 (U.S. Census)	Unknown (estimate – 5)
1940	352 (U.S. Census)	225 (U. of O. Knight Library mine records)
1950	2 (U.S. Census)	3 to 4 (estimate from resident Blair Sneddon)

The 1950 census data listed above is an undercount, as resident Blair Sneddon told me that there were three to four people living in Copia in 1950.

We do not have reliable information about the number of employees of Cornucopia Mines over time. There are a number of employee estimates: given to the author during interviews, in a few newspaper articles, a mine ledger stating the number of employees for two specific years, but few numbers corresponding to the ten year cycle of the U.S. Census. We do not have accurate demographic data for Cornucopia, as far as income or ethnicity, except as given on a single 1920 census page, online.[1]

The 1920 single census page lists 50 of the 242 citizens in Copia. There were more pages, unavailable, for the 1920 census record. The largest majority listed on the census page are, by far, U.S. born. There is a category listing birth place, one for parent's birthplace, and one at the right of the page, labeled "Mother Tongue." There are a total of 50 people recorded on the page. For the column "Mother Tongue": 12 people are listed as German, 2 Danish, 1 Irish, 1 Spanish and 1 Welsh.

Limited archives of the newspaper *Baker City Herald* from the 1930's and 1940's are newly available online. Below are quotes from available articles about the mine and the town of Cornucopia:

"In 1937….The mine increased its gold output by 250 percent." A 1939 news article stated that the mine "had a net profit for 1938 of $122,600."

That profit meant more jobs and more people. Gold ore concentrates in ever greater quantities were being shipped by the mine. The new road, including a part called bootlegger's grade was used to ship to distant smelters. More Baker City newspaper quotes:

"The company is now running the mill for all 3 shifts." (Copia would have had a mini-boom when that occurred.)

"The new drifts (tunnels) are 10 feet high and 8 feet wide. This is to accommodate better drainage and new tracks to handle heavier ore cars…"

"A new solarium, with lights, near the mill, to provide artificial sunshine to miners….for better health….a new ball diamond on the Slum Dam…." In each article, the newspaper gave very positive coverage to the town and company.

There is newly available documentation, online, that the state of Oregon was very helpful to Cornucopia Mines. The state was also indirectly helpful to the population of the town, and the miners of Copia. Oregon Department of Geology and Minerals (DOGM) have recently made available a "historical mining information" section as a link on their webpage. DOGM made many efforts to assist the company and thus the town, as shown in a series of letters from 1939 to 1942. Prior to Pearl Harbor, a new director of DOGM. Chris Dobson wrote to Cornucopia Mines:

"We are looking forward to visiting you….we are supposed, in general, to give (you) whatever service we can….we're pleased to give any cooperation we can with the large operations…" (such as Cornucopia, the best producing mine in the state).

Later in the letter, DOGM General Manager Dobson writes: "One of your assayers applied for a job with our department…" The letter goes on to ask if it is okay for the state of Oregon to give the Copia mine employee a job offer.

Dobson continues: "I would not accept any one of your men and cause you embarrassment…"

In another letter, DOGM suggests that Cornucopia Mines hire a geologist, also letting them know what pay the geologist may expect: "He's single, 49 years old and may get a $175-$200 wage" (monthly?).[2]

I worked as a Business Employment Specialist, also involving counseling and teaching for the state of Oregon Employment Department for ten years. Having served on several state hiring panels, a list could be made of what's currently against state rules during the interchanges quoted above. Trends were different with the hiring process in the 1930's compared to today.

A late December 1941 letter from DOGM (State of Oregon) to Cornucopia Mines, by then closed, asks the mine to look at their assay reports from the smelter in Tacoma. It is suggested that the mine look for documentation of Zinc in the ore. If so, the letter helpfully states, the mine may be able to start up.

Zinc was used for galvanizing, in batteries, and to make brass for war efforts. The state of Oregon was anticipating a federal government shut-down of gold mines, and trying to be very helpful to Cornucopia Mines, and thus the town.[3] There was too little Zinc in their ore to merit re-opening.

U.S. Census for Baker County, 1990 to 2010, average about four percent minority population. This percentage of minority heritage includes Native Americans, Hispanic, Black, Asian and other ethnicity citizens. To compare historic Copia data to recent Halfway data:

The following figures describe citizens of Halfway:

1960 – 505 (U.S. Census)
2000 – 336 (U.S. Census)
2017 – 327 (Hells Canyon Chamber of Commerce)

Another source lists the current population of Halfway at 400 in 2017.

William Carter, in *Ghost Towns of the West*, states "Cornucopia Mine employment swelled to over 700 after the boom of 1884-1885." After more research at the U. of O. Library and the Pine Valley Community Museum, no back up for Carter's 700+ mine employment figure can be found.

Like the start date of the village of Cornucopia, population and mine employee numbers vary. One has to consider that some of the numbers may be derived from the entire area of upper Pine Valley watershed. There were many mines, and several mine mills other than those owned by Cornucopia Mines. The high numbers may also have included everyone living near Copia to the south.

The Halfway population numbers shown are all comparable to several years of Cornucopia's population, over time. At Copia, there is a direct correlation between population and the number of mine employees. Really dubious statistics about Copia's population exist. Lambert Florin, in his book "Ghost Towns of the Pacific Frontier" states that there were "over a thousand people in Cornucopia in the boom' years of 1884-5." No footnote backs up this statement.

---

[1] A single online page, apparently from several, U.S. Census data 1920: freepages.genealogy.rootsweb.ancestry.com/~givens/censusor/or20bk1407 .htm

[2] Oregon Department of Geology and Mineral Industries website. Mining records: www.oregongeology.org/sub/milo/archive/MiningDistricts/ BakerCounty/CornucopiaDistrict/CornucopiaGoldMines.

[3] Ibid.

CHAPTER 5
INTERVIEWS, STORIES, FARM TO TABLE

"In the days of old, the days of gold, how often I remind, in the days of old
When we dug up the gold, in the days of '49"

Traditional song, public domain

WHAT WERE THE RESIDENTS OF COPIA REALLY LIKE? THEY
were a lot like any residents of any small Oregon town. People in
Copia, because of the town's isolation, had to rely more on
themselves. Cornucopians were independent from the rest of the
state. Family ties were quite close.

Heartwarming tales of Copia families are told in the 1980's and
1990's magazines published by the Halfway Community Museum
Pine Valley Echoes and in the *Hells Canyon Journal.* For example, the
1991 Echoes edition has seven small font pages about the pioneer
Pine Valley Crow family. Several members of the Crow family were
miners at Copia. A book could be written about Pine Valley families,
some of them, at times, Cornucopia families. Family tales detail life
both before and after living and working in Copia. Many of the
mining families still live in Pine Valley.

Following are tales told, lately, to the author by some of the few
people still alive who remember the pre-1941 town. The former
citizens of Copia are a golden treasure all by themselves. They paint a
rich portrait of life in a small Oregon mining town.

Copia citizens interviewed tell of townspeople having an easy familiarity. They have a strong bond with others living in the town, all knowing each other. Their hospitality between each other, and with visitors, was proverbial. There were not strict social rules in Cornucopia. In a relatively big city like Baker City there were vague residential groupings of the wealthy, the middle class, and the poor. It appears not so in Copia. In the early days of Copia, up the mountain at the Union Mine, there was the manager's "mansion" and office, also called the big house. When that was abandoned, besides Chris and Jesse Schneider's quality private home, the nicest homes in town were the sixteen company-built miner family homes in Cornucopia.

During the Copia's mining days, a majority of the jobs available in eastern Oregon were lower paying agricultural jobs. The families and single gold miners of Copia could be all called Argonauts, gold searchers. In a larger sense, they were all searching for what we now call family wage jobs.

Many Copia related family stories exist to choose from, detailing life and culture in the town. Most of the tales in this book are family stories gathered first hand. There are not a lot of people left who remember the pre-1941 town.

A list was compiled of gold miner names just during the period 1939-1941, from my collection of miner time cards. There were 81 different last names on the time cards for the time period. All were employees of the mine. Brothers or cousins of the same last name worked in the mine at various times, such as several from the Crow family.

Pine Valley Echoes relates, and the stories here maintain that some families came to the Copia area from the east. Some arrived via the Oregon Trail. Some came by railroad, some by horse or wagon. Some came from the west: from towns like Portland, Baker City and other places.

A very early resident of Cornucopia was Jim Fisk. Jim Fisk Creek flows into Elk Creek, which then flows into Pine Creek at the southern edge of Copia. The creek is named after Jim, a grandson of an Oregon Trail pioneer who arrived by wagon train. Jim was a gold miner at Copia in the early 1900's. Fisk was also a teamster and a wildlife expert.

Teamsters were hired by the government in 1912 to haul Rocky Mountain Elk to areas inside the Wallowas. The Elk arrived via at the closest railroad depot to the north end of the Wallowas. The Elk didn't have first class train seats; they were in horse hauling rail cars. There were few Elk left in the Wallowas at the time. Fisk, and others, hauled the Elk by sleds, in winter, to an area north of Enterprise. It was easier to haul heavy loads over snow. The move was carefully done in early spring, so the Elk would be able to graze somewhat as vegetation poked up through the snow melt. It was reported that the new Elk herd were fed hay bales until most of the snow melted.[1]

When one hikes, or takes a horseback ride into the wilderness up Pine Creek about one half mile north of Copia up, then going east a two or three miles up the steep uphill side of the East Fork of Pine Creek, there is sometimes an Elk herd. If lucky, one can see the herd of Rocky Mountain Elk. This herd was earlier augmented by Fisk and other teamsters, with United States Forest Service's help.

Walk quietly when approaching the herd, or they will spook. The elk bugle, they moo, they hiss and grunt. The elk herds of the Wallowas had been hunted near to extinction by 1912. With government help, Fisk's and others efforts, the elk appear to be making a strong comeback. The elk, too, are part time residents of Cornucopia. Now, there are enough elk to allow hunters to take some during hunting season.

North, and then west up Pine Creek from Copia sits Pine Lakes. The lakes are about five miles northwest from the remote Cornucopia-Mines owned Queen of the West gold mine site. In the alpine forested glacial valley, amongst the granite boulders, beautiful Pine Lakes contain the cobalt blue colors of the sky. The lakes are a treasure of Eagle Cap Wilderness. Early residents of Cornucopia, like Betty and Paul, hiked up to Pine Lakes, upon occasion.

Betty Willett and Paul Fitch

Betty and Paul are kind, warm, forthcoming brother and sister. At ages 93 and 84, they have amazingly good memories. The siblings grew up, in part, at Cornucopia during the 1930's. Paul and Betty lived in Cornucopia approximately from 1934 to 1940. They were not born in Copia.

Betty achieved a 32 year career working as an Administrative Supervisor for Lane County Juvenile Department. Paul also had a solid 32 year career with Consolidated Freightways in various jobs.

Their father, Les Fitch, worked for Cornucopia Mines on and off during the 1930's. The interview was held at Betty's home in Eugene,

Oregon. Permission was granted from both to use their quotes.

Betty: "I hunted with my father once in a while. I shot, I guess three deer. Dad hunted deer and elk. He was a good hunter. We ate a lot of meat. Dad built our house behind the jail, and another separate 'sleeping house' nearby. Both houses, I think, are still there."

Paul: "Dad also built a wonderful merry-go-round, based on a stump behind our house, really fun to play on."

Betty: "Dad was a World War I Marine veteran. He was gassed, and suffered from PTSD, although we didn't call it that at the time. One time, when we were having a meal in our house, the mine set off an explosion of some kind. This set Dad off track. He stumbled out of the cabin and down the road a ways, in a daze, before he realized where he was. This was PTSD. In addition to working for the mine as both a miner and blacksmith helper, Dad ran a restaurant and bar below our cabin, next to the jail. At the Fountain Candy Store (about three businesses away from his restaurant), Dad would play poker. A poker room was set up in the back room of the candy store. He usually won."

The idea of a poker room at the back of a candy store is rich. The town's only candy store, the Fountain, was frequented daily by children. In the evenings an illegal high stakes poker game is going on in the back room. Why there? Did Copia's saloons want a "vig" (fee or payoff) from the gamblers? Did this cause some to play in the back room at the Fountain/Candy Store?

Betty continues: "Dad was so good at poker. Later, he won the title to the three story Grand Hotel in the mining town of Granite (a gold mining ghost town about 70 miles west from Copia). The hotel was closed, but had an operating saloon open in the first story."

A photo in the Baker County Library online historical archives shows Granite's Grand Hotel to be a well-built, ornate, Victorian looking Oregon gold rush hotel. It is now gone.

Paul: "Dad would also win 'hinkies' at poker. This was what we called the mine company script (paper money). He would give a few hinkies to me. A 5 cent hinkie would but a large ice cream cone at the candy store."

Hinkies, company script, was the name of company issued money used at other large mines on the west coast.

Paul adds: "I remember, once I could drive, Dad asking me to go get supplies for our deer camp. I borrowed Smelcer's (one of two open stores, and also the name of the then closed Keller Hotel) truck and brought back supplies for our hunting party with the store truck. I think that Smelcers was the last business to close in Copia, in the mid-1940's.

"My grandparents came to Pine Valley via the Oregon trail in 1880. They brought, along with family member's wagons, horses to breed and sell. The (transcontinental) railroad was too expensive to travel by."

Betty says; "In Copia, local preachers, one or two each time, on varying Sundays, would visit our mining town, coming from Baker or Halfway. One night, two preachers were walking down Main Street on a Sunday night. One stepped in a deep pot hole in the street and got his shoes and pants muddy. I heard the preacher say, there in the street: 'Where in the hell are we?'….that shocked me, the preacher saying that. On some Sundays, a preacher would preach at Swisher's (formerly Keller's) dance hall.

"Mom told me, and I confirm this, that most of the people in Copia were fairly happy. They were all paid similar, good wages, no jealousies. The women played a lot of bridge during their time off. The two stores, then one, in town, had less inventory than a current 7-11. The Cornucopia Mines Company charged our family some for electricity, not much at all. Dad had a glass jar of small gold flakes that he panned from Pine Creek. The jar contained about three or four ounces of gold."

Just think; there was a small jar of shining, gleaming gold sitting right in Betty's humble family cabin.

"I never saw vegetables grown in 'Copia. It was too high an elevation. Snow lasted until late June. Thin soil, too. Snow came as early as September. So, we couldn't get things growing. People could grow strawberries and rhubarb. Mostly, a few flowers is all. Lots of huckleberry picking."

Paul continues, in answer to a question about moonshine whiskey: "The closest moonshine still to Copia was down in Richland. [Twenty miles south west, the town of Charley Keller's first saloon.] I don't remember any stills in Copia."

The miners called the bootleg "tanglefoot," a name for moonshine also used during the California gold rush.

A question about livestock in Copia: "If you had a horse, or cow, in Copia, it was too expensive to feed it in winter because of the deep snow. So, everyone who had horses moved them down to Halfway each winter. When we lived there, because of expenses, there were no cows in Copia. There was a dairy in Halfway that delivered milk up to Copia three seasons of each year. In the winter, we had to drink canned milk, or go to Halfway to buy fresh milk. No one raised cattle, pigs or sheep in Copia, because of the snows. Dad had a horse in Copia."

Paul, about local fishing: "No fish in Pine Creek in Copia, because of the mining. Our family sometimes would camp over at Clear Creek [four or five miles east of Copia] and catch a lot of fish. Before the dams on Snake River, one could catch Steelhead in lower Pine Creek."

During a recent encounter with a fisherman, he told me that he had just caught a twenty inch trout right in Copia. Much earlier, several invoices in the mine's ledgers document that Salmon was part of the fare served to miners at the mine company cookhouse. Paul indicated that it would have been canned salmon.

Paul: "You couldn't buy fresh fish at Copia for nothing. I would catch small trout in Jim Fisk Creek. We did most of our fishing way downstream Pine Creek, Clear Creek, and East Pine Creek. The limit was ten each. Once in a while a state fish and game officer would be seen around Halfway checking the weirs, to make sure screens were in place to keep the fish from going into the irrigation canals. The officer was a member of Motley family, we were all friends. There were lots of Motleys in Copia."

The Motley family ran the meat market just below the Fitch family houses in Copia on Main Street. Both Paul and Betty state that when they lived in Copia the town residents totally policed themselves, as law enforcement was not seen at Copia.

Paul states: "We didn't have locks on our doors in town. No crime to speak of. When I lived in Halfway in the early 1950's, a state police trooper would drive through town once a week. Their duty was to enforce fish and game laws, like checking to see if fishermen and hunters had licenses. I knew the trooper. He would check my license once in a while. One time, he checked it one week, then, the next week he asked me for it again. I said something like: 'Don't you remember last week?' He said he needed to meet a certain number of license checking for his report to his supervisor."

Paul and Betty stated that when there was a Saturday dance and music at Swisher's Copia Dance Hall, a collection was taken to pay for the dance hall and band. The collection also paid whoever volunteered to be "Sheriff for the night." This person's job was to try to break up the fist fights that occasionally broke out. Paul states that he cannot remember anyone ever being lodged in the Copia jail. The jail was below their house.

Paul indicated that the main job of the mining town's volunteer "'Sheriff for the night" was to make sure no one froze to death if they passed out in the snow, after the dance, and that they somehow got home.

Betty: "There were plays presented as well as dances. We had to entertain ourselves, no TV, no radio. When there was a band, it usually consisted of a piano, fiddle, drum and guitar. It was popular music, like the songs 'Harbor Lights' and 'Oh Johnny.' I would dance, sometimes the jitterbug on faster songs. We'd heat water and have baths every week or so, especially if there was to be a dance that night. Chris Schneider's family band played songs like 'Sally Goodwin and Ragtime Annie.'"

Music and dance were an important part of the social life in Copia. Not just technique and melody, music conveyed bits of history and culture to the citizens. Music could provide some insight into the meaning of life itself. Music, as we know, can invoke joy, beauty or sorrow.

Betty continues: "It was a lot of work to heat the water and use buckets to bathe. We had a postmistress named Rachel Krigbaum, who lived in the back part of the post office. There were few jobs for women in Copia. Gossip had it that, earlier, Mrs. [last name withheld] was the madam of a cat house on the entire third floor of the hotel."

The first post office was immediately to the south of the Fountain Candy Store on Main Street. The last post office was across the street. Post offices were a very important and vital part of isolated mining towns. Miners received family news via the post office, and sent letters about how they were doing to loved family members.

The mine company built the recreation center named Donley Hall. Dances, plays and movies were put on there just from 1939 to 1941. When the mine shut down, so did the new recreation center. After shutdown, parties were still held in the recreation center. Betty confirmed that Charles and Rhoda Sneddon had a key to the building, and would open it for weekend community recreational events. The

Donley Recreation Center had the dance floor, a three lane bowling alley and a barber chair area. Snow crushed the building late in the 1940's.

About the Cornucopia school, Paul: "Locals secured funds from the state to pay the teacher, and run the school. The mine funded the construction of the school. The mine allowed no worker vacations, nor any kind of seniority. So Dad would quit his mine job, and our family would go on vacation each summer after school let out. Then Dad, being a skilled miner, would get rehired upon return from vacation.

"At the mine's community hall, a white sheet would be put up. We watched movies. I remember seeing Disney's Snow White, and King Kong. A lot a sheep and vegetables were farmed in down in Pine Valley, brought up to sell in the Copia stores. We had a good time growing up in Copia.

"For big events like weddings, we went to Boise, Baker City or Halfway. Copia streets were dirt, with a bit of tar and gravel. Chuck holes were patched from a barrel of tar. We got the lid off it, once, and got all tarry. We were taken to the front of Swisher's store. They had a tall hand-pumped gas pump there, and the gas took off the tar off us."

Betty continues: "There was a baseball field on one of the few flat areas of town, the Slum Dam. You can see this area today, near Pine Creek. After we played a game, we'd be covered with powder. The powder itched my arms and burned my face. I didn't play much baseball for that reason."

Betty, at age 93, seemed to have no ill after effects from playing on the toxic – at the time – slum dam baseball field. Paul: "The company doctor, Pollock, came to town twice a week. I don't ever remember needing his help."

Paul answered a question about jokes played: "Dad was born on Halloween, so, it was a double holiday. One of our pranks: that night we would tip over an outhouse so it fell away from the path from the house, exposing the pit. Then, someone would come out of the house to use the outhouse, in the dark, and feeling for the door, fall into the pit where the outhouse used to be."

Betty stated that they used to hike up the mountain to the site of the Union Adit. The kids would explore the then existing mine office and manager's housing building. Nine years ago I was told, stating in the book about Cornucopia Mines, that the "mansion" was torn down soon after the Colter Adit opened in 1936. This was incorrect. Some locals still call the extensive three story foundations "the mansion."

Betty stated that the mine "mansion" was not called that in the 1930's and 1940's, it was called "the big house." The big house was standing until the late 1940's. She related that there were glass enclosed oak bookcases and several interior architectural features still there, when she explored the empty big house.

Betty continues: "The Basque sheep herders would come through town in the summers, and camp nearby once in a while. They would let me ride their horses."

In answer to a question about the noise of the new mine mill affecting Copia, Betty states: "We didn't hear the mine mill, or we got so used to it that we didn't. The mine would sound off a loud whistle when there was an accident. All those years, Dad just went to the hospital in Baker one time, when the skip dropped way too fast inside the mine shaft. He recovered in a few days."

Blair Sneddon

Blair was very kind, in giving full answers to over two hours of questions, and during many calls. Like many in the Pine Valley area, the Sneddons were pioneers, coming east to Pine Valley from Salt Lake City. Blair's memories of Copia are from the latter part of his 17 years there – 1936-1953. Sneddon was born in Utah in 1935. In 1941, when the Copia school closed, Blair moved and went to school in Baker City, coming back to Copia during summers and weekends.

Blair's father was Charley Sneddon, hired to work at and later manage the mine site. Sneddon's management duties started in 1942. Charley worked for the mine as a warehouseman beginning in 1935. Blair's father's duties as mine manager included supervising Chris Schneider and Ann Ingalls father – Sylvester Marker.

These were the only three people the mine kept on full time from 1942 until the early 1950's. Others were hired part time in winter to shovel snow off mine buildings.

Blair: "Dad would make sure the Colter Adit was locked, but able to be opened and entered if needed. He sold the mine company houses [the double row built in the 1930's, on the east side of Pine Creek] and scrap metal from machinery. The houses were cut in half, for hauling down to Halfway.

"After we cut one house, before it was moved, someone stole one of the house halves, hauled it away in the middle of the night. For many nights after that, we would take turns staying up and listening to see if the thieves returned for the other half. After we gave up staying up, they returned and stole the other half. We would look around in Halfway and see if we could spot the stolen house. We didn't find it.

"Earlier, Dad was the chairman of the school board in Copia. There were two rooms in the school, grades one to four and another for grades five to eight. The school did not send any of us to play on the baseball field at the Slum Dam. That was all outside of school hours. The EPA had it wrong about the Slum Dam, it wasn't very toxic. There was no mayor, no city council."

This must have been the case during the time Blair remembers. Earlier, mine blacksmith Chris Schneider stated that in February 1936, he was elected mayor. Schneider was mayor before the time-frame of Blair's memories.

Blair: "After the mine shut down, Dad had the key for the mine recreation hall. On some Saturdays, there would be a dance or a movie or bowling, not a lot of people there. A lot of beer was con-sumed....I was one of the pin setters for the bowling alley in the recreation center. The adults had a game called 'kill the pinsetter,' where once in a while they would send a ball down the lane while I was setting pins."

Ann Ingalls states that, as a pinsetter, she was a victim of the same prank.

Blair: "When the mine was open, the Christmas parties were great. The mine company gave really good presents to each child. My favorite present was a tin train with tracks."

Despite some tales of frozen pipes in winter, Blair remembers the water in their Copia house running in winter, not freezing.

Ann Ingalls

Ann lived in Cornucopia from 1945 to 1951. She has also been very kind giving her time for lengthy phone interviews. Ann gave much help during the walking tour of Copia in 2017. Ann worked for several businesses over the years. One was called "Halfway Stages," which was a fleet of trucks. She performed bookkeeping and account-ting. She advanced to become paymaster for the large construction firm Morrison and Knudsen during the construction of the Snake River dams. Another employer using Ann's bookkeeping skills was the Halfway newspaper *Hells Canyon Journal.*

One of Ann's grandfathers came to Halfway from Wisconsin, the other set of grandparents arrived in Baker. They came from a now vanished Oregon gold town called 'Sticies Gulch.'

She states: "I started school at the Tiedeman School [now known as South Baker Elementary]. We moved to Copia because my parents had just sold the telephone office in Halfway. My dad accepted a job as a caretaker at Cornucopia Mines. We were ready for a move. It was 1945.

"By the time I arrived at our house in Copia, it had a water heater and electricity. The water and power were either free or nearly free. Rent was very low.

"When we got there, the last store had closed. There were no other businesses in town open. We left in 1951 because my parents had bought the Jimtown Store." Jimtown was about halfway between Halfway and Copia.

Ann continues: "My friend Trudy - Jessie Schneider's grand-daughter – and I would run wild all over the town. Chris called us girls 'livestock.' Jessie Schneider served us wonderful wild huckle-berry dumplings. She had picked the berries, and made the dump-lings. She made us wait while she 'spanked' the cream [into whipped cream]. They were the best ever. One Christmas the Schneider's and us didn't exchange gifts on Christmas because Chris left the gifts on his wood chopping block; forgetting them. He went on to do something else.

"Jessie Schneider had one of the only vegetable and flower gardens, about 10 by 20 feet, in Copia. She grew lettuce and a few vegetables. Her flower garden was beautiful."

In answer to a question about encountering any Native Americans, Hispanics, African Americans or other minorities in Copia, Ann answered: "World War II had just ended. The Japanese, to us, were still considered a threat. Trudy and I were playing in Copia, away from home. We knocked on a cabin door and asked for water....[following is a very unusual example of non-friendliness in Cornucopia]....the lady at the cabin said she had to haul water from Pine Creek in buckets, so she would give us none. She suggested we walk down to the creek and drink right from it.

"Pine Creek was totally off limits for us. One child had drowned there, falling in when Pine Creek was raging with spring thaw. But, since the cabin lady told us to go there and drink, we did.

"I look up from my creek drinking, here comes what we thought was a Japanese man. We fled, running home and yelled (in fear) at mom, 'The Japs are coming.' We didn't see that the man had a fishing rod in his hand."

Apparently, by the 1946 date of this encounter, trout had returned to Pine Creek, as the mine had been shut down for over five years.

Ann: "Turns out it was a Chinese man, Jack Eng. Jack was a Baker City restaurant owner of a business named the Royal Cafe. My dad, with me present at the Royal Cafe restaurant, told the embarrassing story of the fishing incident in Copia. He told the story right to Jack Eng. Everybody laughed.

"One winter we were hauling a load of groceries up from Halfway. The team reached the edge of Copia, and could go no more because the snow was so deep. My dad, Sylvester Marker, started wading through the snow. Charley Sneddon drove the sleigh and unhitched the horses from the supplies sled. He put my mom Olive on one horse. He rode the other horse, with me, through the snow up to the mine office apartment and stable. We stayed at the heated [by woodstove] mine office apartment that night. Our house was too cold to stay that night.

"Chris Schneider walked to my dad wearing, and bringing extra snowshoes. That way they could make up to the mine apartment. The horses were taken care of. The next day we unloaded the groceries from the sled. We moved into the warmed up house in Copia. Anybody that needed help in Copia was given it by everyone living there. We all worked together. When someone went to Halfway shopping, they bought for others in town, too.

"We were allowed to go in the mine one time. The dark shaft walls seemed like they were kind of caving in. There was a blast of very cold air coming out of the Coulter."

Ann confirmed that a second gold miner boarding house, to the north of the one that exists today, was connected to the existing one by a second floor walkway. No photos have surfaced of either of the boarding houses when they were occupied by gold miners.

Ann: "It's amazing how many graduates from Halfway High School went into highly skilled professional careers. There were doctors, dentists, teachers, lawyers and other professionals."

Ann's family home no longer exists in Cornucopia.

A motif emerges from the former residents of Copia. People interviewed grew up there in a somewhat hardscrabble situation. They went on to have very successful professional level careers. No silver spoons, no family fortunes, no jobs handed to them. In Cornucopia self-sufficiency, problem solving and teamwork were highly valued. This ethos really helped Ann, Betty, Blair, Bob, and Paul. The same theme was present talking with part time residents Galen, Kerry and Larry.

Managing a Household in Early Copia

An astonishing depth of technological history, and time, is represented here. In the book *Never Done: A History of American Housework*, we learn that it took fifty gallons of water to complete one clothes wash. Indicated in the book, four hundred pounds of water was needed for one complete wash cycle, including the rinse. That's a lot of work, hauling that water by buckets from Pine Creek to a cabin. These hard working pioneers not on the town's water system hauled drinking, wash, bath and cooking water in buckets. Water, for the woman in Ann's tale, was heated on a wood stove. We assume that she had to split and store wood and kindling.

Later, a more labor efficient method was employed using water heating coils wrapped around the woodstove. A giant technological advantage was having an electric water heater in your house for the first time, a huge labor saving device.

Consider labor saving devices in your closets and garages. We all have numerous electric appliances and tools. You have perhaps a dozen electric gadgets that get used about once a year. These were bought at considerable cost to make your life easier. Think how much more work Cornucopians had to do, when the only appliance in the house was the wood stove. An advancement for the time was some kind of clothes washing bucket that had a ringer above. How about being present when the first water was piped into your Copia cabin, or when you first got copper water coils wrapped around the woodstove for heating water?

Dale Taylor, Cousin Bob Taylor

The Taylors are a Pine Valley family with strong connections to Copia. We think of the business of provisioning towns like Copia, now, as part of the "farm to table" continuum. Cornucopia could not provision itself, at that altitude, with the heavy snowfall each winter. The town needed lots of supplies. This need was an ongoing basis. The Taylor family was part of the chain of supply the mining town relied upon.

Floyd and Marcella Taylor were married in 1933. Both Taylors were later volunteers for the Pine Valley Community Museum. Marcella's mother was Jesse Mitchell, an ancestor of author John Updike. There was a family member named Monroe Updike. Updike marched through Georgia with General Sherman and his army of Union soldiers. Updike was one of the locators of both Queen of the West and Red Jacket Mines, later bought by Cornucopia Mines. For a while, dates unknown, Monroe worked for Cornucopia Mines. The Taylors, like many in Pine Valley, had a family member who served in the Civil War.

My middle name is an old family last name, Taylor. William Taylor was my great grandfather. I am no relation to the Taylors of Pine Valley. The Taylors in my family were also western pioneers, founding the town of North Bend, Washington. My great grandfather also marched through Georgia with Gen. Sherman and Monroe Updike during the Civil War. The roots of family trees sometimes intertwine deep underground.

Marcella Taylor's father, Willis, arrived by horseback in Pine Valley from the northern side of the Wallowas in 1896. A Taylor family ancestor, Willis Mitchell was one of the teamsters hauling goods into Copia in the early days. Their home in Halfway was twelve miles from Copia.

Floyd Taylor's father, John Taylor, working for the railroad, arrived in Oregon around 1885. The Taylors, at times, were teamsters hauling goods and ranchers. They were also involved in wagon freighting ore from Copia to the closest rail head in Robinette, on the Snake River. Then the wagons were filled with goods bound for Cornucopia. The Taylors made sure that they had a paying load to haul to and from Copia.

One of Floyd Taylor's sons, Dale Taylor, is now president of the

Pine Valley Community Museum in Halfway. The hard working volunteer museum staff is instrumental with preservation efforts in Copia. The wonderful Halfway based museum houses Cornucopia artifacts and other aspects of local history, including farming and ranching life in Pine Valley.

Floyd Taylor's brother George Taylor was the father of last baby born in Copia – Bob Taylor. George Taylor came to Copia and started work in the mines in 1938. Bob Taylor's father, George, met his future wife Claudean at one of the Saturday night mine recreation center dances. Claudean's sister worked as a cook for Cornucopia Mines. Claudean arrived in Copia about the same time as George Taylor.

Bob Taylor lived briefly in the Taylor family log cabin in 1941. Bob's mother Claudine delivered her baby with the help of the Cornucopia's Dr. Pollock. The Taylors left the log cabin soon after the birth of Bob. When the mine closed, they moved to Halfway. The log cabin is now owned by Galen West.

A retired Professional Land Surveyor, Bob lives in Halfway. He has helped with the walking tours of Copia, and provided me with information about Copia. Bob provided a plat map of the town serving as a basis for the attached map of Copia. The plat map has lots but no buildings indicated.

Kerry Gulick

Kerry is the great, great nephew of Chris Schneider. Kerry first came to Copia as a youngster in 1962. Kerry and his family currently own the former Schneider home, the most ornate, largest homes of the surviving pre-1941 structures. Over several summers, as a child, Kerry spent about a cumulative total of a year living in Chris and Jesse's Copia home. The Gulicks later inherited the house.

Part of Kerry's background was as a miner in Copia for United Nuclear in the early 1980's. He also mined for several years in Nevada. He is currently raising cattle and running an excavation company in Halfway.

Kerry states: "Starting in the mid 1940's, Chris was a paid caretaker for ten or fifteen years, and then he worked as a volunteer caretaker at the mine. I've seen him confront window breaking vandals at mine buildings, he ran them right off. He used his blacksmith skills to make lots of hardware, including his own gate hinges. He saved bent nails, then straightened them out. His forge was in an outbuilding by the house, fired by coal, small but like the forges up at the mine. It's still there. He retired from blacksmithing, doing very little of it when I was there.

"Chris and Jessie were very kind to the tourists, and loved to talk about the mine. One story I heard from my Uncle Calvin [a miner for Cornucopia Mines] was about some miners on an upper level inside the mine. Near where they were working, there was the open end of a core sample drilling hole."

Core sampling is a very important mine task, strongly affecting profit or loss. Miners drill a two or more inches round hole into the mountain and extract the round of rock from the hole. The round segments of core sample rock, up to 5 feet long, are analyzed by the assay office staff to see how much gold, if any, is in the sample. These findings determine where new mining areas should be blasted out, or not. A core sample can be taken in any direction underground. In this story, the core sample hole went about 100 feet vertically down all the way down to end at the next level (tunnel), a lower level.

Kerry went on to explain that miners know that core sample holes could be very dangerous. If miners were blasting near a core sample hole that went all the way into other open workings in the mine, rocks could shoot out of the other end of the core sample hole somewhat like bullets from a gun.

Kerry continues: "When they were done with drilling, sometimes these miners would make ghostly noises down an old core sample hole, like 'wooo....wooo...' It happens that the noises were heard by a newly hired miner working on the lower level. He was listening near his end of the core sample hole. He got scared and quit his job.

"Before it collapsed, I was allowed in the Coulter Tunnel. Chris [Schneider] had the keys to all the mine buildings and the mine itself. Going underground, as a youngster, was a dream comes true. There were steep ore chutes coming down from above, poor ventilation. I could see places where the gold vein pinched out so narrow that you couldn't put your hand in it. I could see specks of gold in some of the ore, and I got a bit of it.

"Working in the [new as of late 1970's] Keith adit, we punched air ventilation holes up to the surface as we drilled in. UNC put in a 'step up' compressor to run the drills. We did core sampling. The samples were one inch in diameter and several feet long. We gave the samples to the geologists [including Larry Bush] to test if the rock had gold in it. As a kid, I sold used core samples to the tourists at Copia."

Kerry then spoke of his relative Chris Schneider, and the Schneider home. "[Great great] Uncle had steely grey blue eyes, a German background, he could have a look that would melt you. He was kind of strict; you didn't cross him at any time. He added on to his house over time. He built a structure between the washroom behind the house, and the outhouse, called dog heaven. Cat heaven was in the woodshed. But I don't remember Chris or Jesse ever having pets."

The structures behind the house, with the snow weight, began to tilt and lean against the backside of the Schneider/Gulick home. Heaven forbid – the dog and cat heavens had to be demolished to save the house.

Kerry continues: "Chris and Jesse would have had their first water heater in the 1930's or 1940's. It was a coil that wrapped around the woodstove that went into a tank. Several homes in Copia had this set up.

"The town's water came from a tank up-hill a bit above town on the west side of Pine Creek. The tank was fed by a spring north of Elk Creek. That system may still work at our house [the former Schneider house]. The water has not been turned on there in years. The pipes run under Main Street. We lost power to the house when the mine power house was caved in by snow. The house is now lighted by kerosene and back to wood heating. The State of Oregon tried to give the road out front to the county. They wouldn't take it."

The State of Oregon Department of Transportation still owns Copia's Main Street. Along with some help from adjacent landowner USFS, the street has been re-surveyed. They seem to be planning on changing and making their Main Street different and wider, hornswoggling slices of land from some of the lot owners in Copia.

Some of the front yard of Galen West's log cabin lot, or some of the historic Schneider/Gulick front yard, or other lot pieces could be taken. Why? Perhaps the Oregon Department of Transportation and USFS planners foresee a bustling future four lane Cornucopia Main Street. Wouldn't it be a nightmare to see a wide paved Main Street with an ugly Starbucks between Galen's log cabin and the Schneider/

Gulick home? A new coffee building in Copia would architecturally look like, as they all do, a giant electric razor.

"Barista, I'll have a skinny tall triple pumpkin spice ghost town Frappuccino."

Not for me.

Serious scares exist for Cornucopia. A forest fire burned near to Copia in the early 1980's. Kerry states he worked as an equipment operator for the fire crew. The fire crew wrapped the two-story Schneider home with fire proof material. This possibly saved the home from being ignited by flying sparks.

Kerry told a very believable Copia ghost story, related later.

---

[1] Wallowa Valley Chieftain: www.wallowa.com/20070831/wapiti-brought-back-to-wallowas-with-great-effort-fanfare.

CHAPTER 6
MINING TOWN CRIME

"Just then a bolt of lightning, struck the courthouse out of shape
While everybody knelt to pray, the drifter did escape"

"Drifter's Escape" by Bob Dylan, copyright Columbia Records, 1968

RARELY WAS THERE MAJOR CRIME IN CORNUCOPIA. MUCH less crime compared to other Wild West mining towns like Copperfield. No hanging tree, no boot hill, no cemetery at all. Combined with the self-policing character of the citizens of Copia, we have the notion of a fairly safe town. One could view bootleg whiskey and prostitution as major crime in Copia. If you are employed by the IRS, non-taxed bootlegging and prostitution would appear to be a major crime. Around 1915, about 25% of federal revenue was derived from liquor taxes. From a federal frame of reference there was quite a bit of crime in Cornucopia. The operative word here is "major."

In one view, lacking blindness or even death due to faulty moonshine, alcoholism, uncured venereal disease, or people too young to be involved in promiscuous activities, these two crimes could be classified as not major. The crime examples, with the exceptions noted, are often considered victimless crimes. Nearly all gold mining towns had bootleg whiskey and prostitution challenges. In some mining towns, these crimes caused great harm.

Little criminal harm occurred in Cornucopia. In hours of research on this topic, four instances of major crime at Copia can be found between 1885 and 1950. There is also one instance of a major criminal coming from Copia and an arson fire in the late 1970's. Miner Dale Holcomb told a tale he heard about a miner stabbed in the 1920's, no other details available. The shooting described earlier occurred a few miles from town.

We sometimes enjoy tales of the western outlaw character. The image of an outlaw allows us, in our private musings, to identify with the outlaw. We can be either worse or better than we actually are.

Starting in the late 1880's, a gang of robbers and murderers called the McCarty gang operated around the edges of the Wallowa Mountains. Not to paint the McCarty gang as outlaw-folk heroes, they were clearly plain old criminal outlaws. One of the McCarty gang members came from Cornucopia.[1] There is no reported crime in Copia connected with the McCarty gang. Crime was perpetrated by the McCarty's close by. This gang's out of town activities are not counted here as major Cornucopia crime.

The Eastern Oregon based McCarty outlaw gang were no Robin Hood or Butch Cassidy type of gang. With the proceeds from their first bank robberies, they purchased small distressed ranches on the outskirts of the Wallowas. They also bought a couple of ranches east into Idaho and western Utah. They would rob and often murder. Then hide out at the most remote of their ranches from the crime site, pretending to ranch while things cooled down. They were wannabe ranchers; posers and charlatans.

The nearest major crime to Copia by the McCartys was the robbery of the mining town Sparta store. This store was the main business in town, about 25 miles southwest of Copia. There was no bank at the now ghost town of Sparta. Or the gang would have robbed it, too. At the Sparta crime at least no one, unlike several victims of their other robberies, was shot. The McCarty's not only robbed the store, but individually each local in the store at the time.[2] It is not known where the gang hid out after their Sparta crime spree.

The McCarty ranch hideout north of the Wallowas was known to be in a large area known as "Robber's Roost." Much later, for about ten years, musician John Fogerty had a remote river front vacation home built near the Robber's Roost area. The house sits near the town of Troy. Fogerty sold the house, it became a vacation rental. One can rent the house; sit on his former river front deck singing his lyric: "Rolling, rolling, rolling on a river." By Fogerty's time, the

McCarty's had long ago been either shot or brought to justice.

Crime in Copia: Five miners were arrested and tried in Baker City for "high grading" (stealing) gold from the mine. Miles Potter states that the Cornish miners were especially skilled at high grading gold.[3] This was reported in the news to be a major crime problem for the mine. There was some free gold, gold you could see in the mix of ore that was milled. Once in a while, free gold nuggets were found in the mine. Two of the gold thieves were convicted and jailed in Baker City. They were selling their stolen gold in Baker City. The most interesting crime story out of Copia is the tale of outlaw Six Shooter Carnahan.

Six Shooter Carnahan sported one or two pearl handled revolvers. One story has him usually wearing his guns in his holsters, and sometimes in his boot. Carnahan was reported to be often under the influence of local bootleg liquor. He worked, at times, for Cornucopia Mines.

An ostentatious scheme of stealing his employer's office safe was launched by Six Shooter and a sidekick. This was while he worked for the Copia mine. Carnahan stole the safe and lit out down the mountain. Half way towards Halfway, they dynamited the safe open. Carnahan was caught; the fate of his accomplice is unknown.

The following fits in with a kindness narrative about the Cornucopia Mining Company. The mine representative at the trial in Baker City told the judge to "go easy on Carnahan." Over time, the company generally behaved in an altruistic but very business-like manner towards their employees. Apparently Six Shooter was a good employee. The mine management viewed the safe theft incident as an isolated character flaw. Perhaps he was drunk at the time. Carnahan was not lodged in the Copia jail, but at the jail in Baker City.

Six Shooter's great, great nephew Chet Carnahan stated that Six Shooter lived most of his life in a small community, near Halfway, called Carson. Chet confirmed that his relative was well liked by everyone locally, including the management of Cornucopia Mines. Six Shooter was not well liked in Idaho. According to Chet, family tales tell that he occasionally went to perform robberies in Idaho, returning to hide out in Carson. This 'rob and hide out' was the same M.O. used by the McCartys.

Chet Carnahan stated that Six Shooter was not married. Another historical source states that he was married. Carnahan's robber hideout and eventual home location was about five miles south of Cornucopia. It might seem tempting to research where he lived. Then, obtain land owner permission to do some searching with a metal detector. This has probably already been done. A very high probability exists that any gold buried by Six Shooter, if any ever was, is long gone. No buried pirate treasure.

A final example of major crime in Copia is the late 1940's theft of a house in Copia. That's right, a house. Blair Sneddon's tale was told previously.

Kerry stated that former Copia Mayor Chris Schneider never mentioned crime, shootings or any murders at Cornucopia. Schneider did mention to Kerry jailing drunken miners and cowboys for a night in the Copia jail to sober up.

The main reason there were no gold robberies from gold shipped out of Cornucopia Mine is that most of the gold shipped was either unrefined "sponge" gold cones or gold mixed with other minerals. Both these needed to be further refined at a smelter. Minerals shipped to the smelter were in barrels or sacks of concentrates. Earlier, there must have been some pure gold bricks shipped from the mine. This was evidenced by the story of the brick of gold on the bar at Keller's Hotel.

There you have it. Between 1885 and the 1960's, just four Copia major crimes can be found – plus the 1970's arson. Just like clockwork, every twenty years there is major crime in Cornucopia. Be ever vigilant and watch out, current citizens of Copia. Don't even go to sleep like the Sneddons needed to do. Like before, during the night time house stealing (not horse stealing) criminals might strike and haul off one of the lodge cabins. Or even worse, steal a cabin with you sleeping in it. A major crime is long over-due! Where is that sheriff, anyway? Joking aside, this Copia trend of being law abiding does not seem like a stereotypical Wild West mining town.

The mostly unused Copia jail is on the National Register of Historic Places. The jail is in good condition, considering its age. The punishing effects of Cornucopia's winter snows don't show. The jail is the tribal elder of all public structures in the town. Any records as to whom and how many were incarcerated in the Copia jail are missing. The Pine Valley Community Museum is in charge of restoration efforts at the Copia jail. My Cornucopia Mine book helped fund some of the cost of a new jail roof. Restoration work is on an ongoing basis at the Copia jail. An ongoing need for funding exists.

On the front of the jail is a sign identifying the structure. Currently, at the back of the jail lot is a safe we found nearby in 2016, half buried. The find was at the site of the Keller Hotel. More information is in the Afterward about finding the safe. Throughout the town the crime of vandalism has been a pernicious and persistent problem in Copia.

A challenge at the jail and the Schneider/Gulick home will be to prevent vandals from breaking in the doors or damaging the structures. Our history belongs to all of us, not just the vandals. If you are in Cornucopia and observe someone committing an act of vandalism, please record the license plate and call 911.We need to serve as volunteer Sheriffs to help preserve what's left in the town. There is cell phone service at and near the lodge.

---

[1] *Outlaw Tales of Oregon*, Jim Yuskavitch, Globe Pequot Press, 2007, page 87.

[2] Ibid., page 85.

[3] *Oregon's Golden Years*, Miles Potter, Caxton Printers, 1987, page 152.

CHAPTER 7
PHOTOS

"Glad 2 C U"

Welcoming inscription on Chris and Jesse Schneider's
front gate at their Copia home

1914 Main Street in Cornucopia.

Store in Halfway that helped supply Cornucopia.

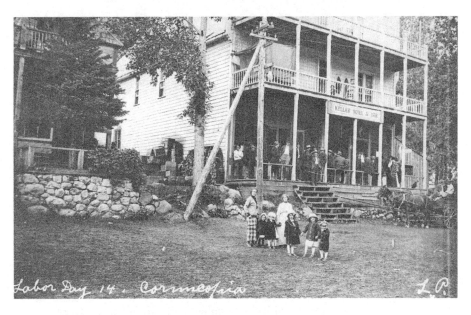

Keller Hotel and Bar. Main Street, Copia.

Holiday parade in front of Keller Dance Hall. Main Street, Copia.

Town people watching a Labor Day rock drilling contest
in front of Keller's Hall.

1912 Labor Day baseball game on future Slum Dam site.

Town people in front of Candy Store-Fountain.

Main Street saloon, 1950's, possibly called "The Cornucopia."

Inside a Copia general store, likely Brown and Pierce on Main Street.

Cornucopia stage coach in front of Keller Hotel.

A couple riding in the Last Chance Mine ore tramway, likely then owned by
Cornucopia Mines.

Workers inside Cornucopia Mines Union Mine Mill.

All photographs above are courtesy of Baker County Library.

Cornucopia Mine, Cornucopia, Oregon.

Copia family in front of snow cave leading into their cabin. Dressed up for the mine's Christmas party? (Author's collection.)

1888 Stock Certificate for corporation then owning Cornucopia Mines. (Author's collection.)

Gold miner boarding house in Cornucopia. (Author photo.)

Author in front of Schneider house.

Ann Ingalls in front of her parents' house.

Cornucopia Jail
(Wikimedia/Ian Poellet)

DANCE
Cornucopia
Community Club
DONLEY HALL

Date April 29

Music by BETTER-Half

Admission $1.25

Flyer for a dance at Copia's Donley Recreation Center.
(Courtesy of Pine Valley Community Museum.)

CHAPTER 8
UNEXPLAINED EVENTS: 'CREEPY COPIA?'

"Cause they got to ride forever, on that range up in the sky
On horses snorting fire, as they ride on, hear their cries"

"Ghost Riders in The Sky" by Stan Jones, 1948, public domain

A CREDIBLE GHOST ENCOUNTER IS TOLD BY BLAIR SNEDDON. Ghostly sounds that he heard several times upstairs in Copia's Keller Hotel:

"It was well known that Keller's [empty] Hotel was haunted. We would sneak in there and go through the rooms. I heard that there was a whorehouse on the upper floor. There were the normal noises of an old empty wooden hotel. Upstairs, I would hear different, scary sounding noises. These were sounds like bumps in several of the rooms. Spooky carved lions were carved on the barroom pool table legs."

Ann lngalls states that in her time at Copia, several times sneaking into the empty Keller Hotel, she heard no ghostly sounds. The hotel was boarded up to the public. Galen West states that during all his time in the Keller, he heard no ghostly noises. This is not to diminish Blair's experience at all.

Kerry Gulick related another believable ghost story, witnessed by several people, about his Cornucopia house – the Schneider home.

"When our kids were young, my wife hosted a girl scout troop for a sleep over at the Schneider place. My wife heard someone walking on the porch with a shuffle, but there was no one there. It turned out that what she heard sounded just like the way Chris Schneider [by then gone] would walk. I went to the porch and imitated his walk. My wife said 'you nailed it.'"

Kerry then told his wife that was the way he heard Chris Schneider walk in years past.

Kerry continues: "Later, a nephew that stayed with us described the same, mysterious shuffling sound event. I had not told him about Chris's shuffle step, or about my wife hearing it."

Interestingly, both Kerry and Blair's Copia tales tell of hearing, not seeing, a ghost.

During the writing of the first Cornucopia Mine book, no credible ghost tales had been related to me. In the book Afterword, I tell a story about walking up to the Schneider home around 2009. Standing on the porch Kerry described, knocking on the door, stating: "I didn't really expect Chris Schneider to greet me....being dead for nearly 30 years." Clearly no one was there when I first approached the house. No one answered my loud knocks, I thought. While taking the few steps from porch toward the gate, I felt a "sudden and sharp urge to do something positive." One of Chris' carved gate posts was lying in the small front yard. I propped it back up with rocks, my positive act. We all have positive urges, some of us more than others. Where did my urge come from?

If one mined into Chris Schneider's strong but positive and helpful psyche, Kerry states that there was a consistent decades-old desire to see Cornucopia Mines reopen. Who knows, that desire could have carried on into some kind of afterlife. Provided there is one. Following are comments, some snarky, describing doubtful ghostliness in Copia.

Wikipedia misinforms: "Cornucopia has a reputation as a ghost town due to the deaths that occurred there....A ghost town reputation....a few killings over the years..." I can find no other source, no documentation from Wikipedia that lists murders at any time in Copia.

Wikipedia rambles on: "Cornucopia has become a tourist attraction for those looking for a creepy thrill."[1] Creepy implied like a commercial Halloween haunted house with fake blood, killer clowns and monsters popping out?

Why, anonymous writer quoted in Wikipedia, did you not give details of even one of the many mysterious deaths or murders at Copia? An epidemic of violence is inferred here. We know that several miners died in the mines at Copia over the years, like in any large mine. After all, in every single town, every single person dies sometime. Are all towns creepy?

The *Oregonian* writer Doug Perry wrote a Halloween article in 2016. The headline: "Rich, even murderous history can still be found in Oregon's ghost towns." Below that headline the first word of the article is: "Cornucopia…" The sentence goes on to list other Oregon ghost towns. More was written about scary events and murders at the other ghost towns. None of the story examples occurred in Cornucopia. The impression created is that Copia, together with other ghost towns, is murderous and dangerous. It's a Halloween story, after all. Feel the BOOO!!

"Eight Creepy Oregon Ghost Towns " is an article title from the website "Only In Your State." Cornucopia is listed as the number two creepiest ghost town in Oregon. Well, rated as the number two creepiest in the state, indeed. What are the criteria for creepiness? Why not award Copia #1 creepiest?

Another ghost town website states "Visit [Cornucopia] this ghost town at your own risk."[2] Will we be attacked by angry ghosts upon arriving in Copia? Will it be like the violent parts of the Ghost Busters movies? The authors of these websites and articles just want lots of people to click and read. They use lead words: "creepy, own risk, deaths or murderous." In this bogus vein, this book could have been titled: *Creepy, Murderous, Deathly Cornucopia, Oregon* in a crass attempt to get more book buyers.

There is very little that one could construe as creepy about Copia. There are the tales of ghostly sounds from Blair and Kerry. These encounters don't seem to be creepy. I would welcome another possible, vague, mini-encounter with the spirit of Chris Schneider. Besides being stern when needed, Schneider was well known for a lifetime of kindness and charity. Please tell me, Chris, if there is a heaven. There could be dogs and cats in heaven, too. Pets are so full of love. The "cat and dog heaven" sheds at your former house had to be torn down. Their spirits could be with Schneider, now.

Two real bogeymen at Cornucopia are fire and snow. It is scary, and creepy, that the entire town could easily be wiped out by a forest fire. Or, that the few remaining historical structures could be knocked down by snow. Of course snow and fire can help the forest, too.

Documented, at most, were from eight to ten fatalities at Cornucopia Mines over 50 years. Most all of the mining accident deaths occurred up the mountain at the Union Adit. Mining is one of the more dangerous occupations of all. Mining history book *Drills and Mills* states "in 1910, a hard rock miner was ten times more likely to be killed on the job than his manufacturing counterpart."[3] This ratio indicates a very scary occupation with death as a possibility. The industrial accidents at Copia resulting in death occurred long ago.

In 1935, before it was totally blasted through, the Coulter was first connected to the Union Mine workings from below. The lower levels of the old workings were flooded. Miners drilled very carefully placed small holes at the end of their new adit. The drills connected to the lower workings of the upper Union Adit. The drainage of the old lower levels was started. The mine engineers knew that if suddenly connected by a large opening, there would be a dangerous flood down the tunnel. With a sudden flood they could lose the crew and the timbering in the new Coulter Adit.

The lower workings were mainly drained. One miner was sent down from above, then another, from the Union Adit. The mine engineers wanted to check the holes connecting the workings draining out of the bottom of the older Union mine workings. Near the new connection, sadly, both miners died due to bad air. Their bodies were hauled up through the mine and out from the Union Adit, up the mountain. The body hauling surely must have been creepy, for all concerned. That is a total of four miner deaths, over the years, in the lower portion of the entire Union mine, including the Coulter Adit.

Two Copia stories relate how a teamster and a trucker lost control of their vehicles, crashed and perished near Copia. The last employee fatalities that can be found were due to a blast inside the mine that killed two miners. The 1939 blast was above the town far inside the Coulter Adit.

In all my visits and stays at Copia, there was no scariness. One time I accepted a ride from a kindly hunter, down Cornucopia Mountain to my camp in Cornucopia. The scary ride was on the terrible road from the Union Mine site. The hunter had been drinking to excess.

Nothing seems evident that's creepy about Copia. Unless you made the great mistake and illegal act of crawling into one of the tiny, flooded Cornucopia Mine openings up near the Union Adit. That would be an extremely risky, creepy, and likely, your last and fatal mistake. Either a cave in or bad air could easily kill you. The living mountain is healing itself from mining activity. Mine adits are private property, no trespassing. Don't go in for that reason alone. It's unlikely that the county search and rescue team would risk their lives by crawling in to find your body in an old mine.

It's understandable that Copia's empty, windowless, leaning, two story miner's boarding house could be seen by some as spooky. Yet, the boarding house is an Oregon cultural treasure. It is one of the last four or five intact historical gold miner boarding houses in somewhat good condition left in the state. Perhaps we can start a fund to brace up the building, to save it from falling over. That would be scary if we lost the boarding house.

An example of a truly creepy ghost town is illustrated by a recent story in the *Oregonian* newspaper. The article is about the empty Japanese town of Fukishima. It is a true ghost town. Abandoned because of radioactivity throughout the area due to the nearby Tsunami destroyed nuclear power plants. The article describes a very aggressive, unafraid of humans, radioactive, hungry and feral herd of wild boars. They roam the empty streets of Fukishima. *That* is a creepy and scary ghost town.

Nearby Greenhorn, Oregon is listed on the "Eight Creepy Oregon Ghost Towns" website as the sixth creepiest site in the state. I've spent a full day in the Greenhorn area, looking for one of the few remaining gold miner boarding houses. The boarding house was eventually found about five winding miles over very bad roads. The boarding house is at the hard-to-find and caved in Roberts Mine. The boarding house and cookhouse combined is large two story log structure has been mostly caved in by snow. Not in good shape at all. Remains of the huge cook stove can be seen below a pile of rotting logs. The site is owned by USFS.

Like Cornucopia, mining ghost town Greenhorn has no creepy to be found. The town is missing even an old graveyard. Not that a graveyard is always creepy. The central business district of Greenhorn once had, according to photos, 15 to 20 businesses. They are all gone except for one of the business buildings in ruins. Like Copia, it's hard to understand why Greenhorn is on the 'creepy ghost towns' list. In Greenhorn, there are just two or three miner's cabins left from the old days, and some newer cabins. Not much left, there.

One of the few cabins in Greenhorn is the well preserved, historic and previous summer home of author-dentist Miles Potter. Miles wrote the detailed book *Oregon's Golden Years* about Oregon gold mining history. The book is highly recommended for those interested in Oregon mining history.

On a luminous morning at the only occupied structure to be found in Greenhorn, I knocked on the door of the trailer. Smoke was curling from a chimney. There was a fairly new pickup truck parked outside. A man in camo threw the door open and barked loudly at me: "Hands up!!!" My hands instantly shot upward. Map, writing pad and pen flew into the air like birds.

This was scary Eastern Oregon folk humor. He immediately laughed, as did someone inside, and invited me in. I could dimly see an old man sitting at the breakfast table. They did not appear to be creepy ghost town monsters, inviting me in so they could kill me. Please, don't murder me.

I went right in, sat down to have coffee and pancakes with the deer hunters. Good food, too. I explained myself as, at that time, a teacher on summer vacation. My hobby was explained; to find and record historical Oregon mining town bunkhouses and other struc-tures. Inside were a son and his elderly father. They invited me to stay and talk history. It was pointed out on my map the location of the Roberts Mine, with the bunkhouse. There is nothing creepy about Greenhorn, just plain friendliness. It was a scary ghost town, only during the brief "hands up" prank.

The publically funded website "Travel Oregon" states: "Cornucopia....wild and wooly gold mining full of shootings, saloons, and sporting ladies..." Partly true, certainly there were lots of saloons and sporting women. The "full of shootings" phrase has no supporting documentation. The shootings theory is full of holes. It doesn't carry water. Perhaps the spurious information was taken from Wikipedia. The only information source listed on the "Travel Oregon" site is named "Ghost Towns USA." Once at that website, one also finds no back up for the "full of shootings" statement. The

Copia shootings references were possibly from someone's accurate memory of target practice by the many hunters in the town. These on line statements seem to be an expository and fabricated history of Cornucopia. There are, still, other mysteries about Copia to consider.

A séance was held at Cornucopia in 2009. It was held by members of B.O.S.S. – "Believers of Oregon Spirit Society." An interview aired on KGW TV on July 22nd 2009 featuring B.O.S.S. leader Madonna Merced.[4] Madonna has a fine, detailed and very professional webpage for B.O.S.S. She indicated to me, among other comments, that "Cornucopia is a ghost town full of spiritual residents….spirits who cursed…."

Madonna answered all my questions via several emails about her ghostly event in Copia. She stated that her team recorded lots of "EMF" sensor readings and recordings of ghost cursing at the caved in Cornucopia adit (tunnel). She said that there were many psychic disturbances at the mineshaft.

Like my book about Cornucopia Mine, Madonna was also incorrect about the location of the Coulter adit. The caved in adit (tunnel) we now see is not the Cornucopia Mine Companies Coulter adit, but a new entrance created by United Nuclear in 1980 called The Keith. The newer caved in adit just looks really old by now.

The real Coulter adit location is about 200+ yards south of this site. There is no mining wreckage remaining in this little valley that held the historic 1930's Coulter adit. The tiny valley containing the Coulter has been reclaimed by trees and underbrush. One cannot tell there were a mine entrance and several buildings there. The valley goes westward into the mountain for about 200 yards, ending at a steep slope going uphill. This entire site is on private property and requires permission to enter. Larry Bush indicated that there were no serious accidents at the new adit, the Keith, where Madonna held her séance. United Nuclear stopped all work at the mine in 1982.

The gold mining ghost town of Bourne is about 60 miles, as the crow flies, west from Cornucopia. In 2013 the science fiction television channel SYFY produced, for a national audience, several shows based near Bourne, Oregon, called "Ghost Mine." The Crescent (ghost) Mine is in the Elkhorn Mountains. That gold mine, the towns of Bourne and Sumter were filming sites for the "Ghost Mine" television shows.

The Crescent mine was being operated by the mine owner and

just two miners. The SYFY television group hired three more Oregon gold miners to supplement the existing crew for the television shows. I am acquainted with two of the hired miners, Duck and Richard Secord. Duck is Richard's father. They both seem to be very serious and truthful men. Duck and Richard have been hired by USFS to weld bars at the openings of several mines. This is done for public safety and to protect bat habitat.

Earlier, I spent an afternoon with the Secords. They kindly showed me their gold mine workings in Bohemia's Champion Mine. The Champion Mine goes back over 100 years.

Elkhorn Mountains Crescent Mine, inside and out, was the site of several of the Ghost Mine episode scenes. The television crew filmed with special infrared filters what appeared to be the glowing moving blob of what looked to be a ghost. The blob was perhaps real, perhaps not, deep in the tunnel. The mine's tommy knockers were quite real to miner Duck Secord. He was filmed, outside the mine during a crew meeting, quitting the crew and the TV show. Quitting due to what he said were actual tommy knockers, ghosts that he had perceived in the mine.

We have a reliable source – gold miner Duck Secord – saying there are tommy knockers in the Crescent Mine. He was not verifying the reality of a blob that was supposedly recorded and filmed. The SYFY television channel showed a seemingly spurious ghost like-blob that fits in with the plot of the show. It is the Science *Fiction* channel, after all.

Wildly spooky and violent Cornucopia is a western myth. Throughout numerous internet searches for various wordings like "Shootings at Cornucopia," "Murders at Cornucopia," etc., no specific instances of those types of events can be found. Debunking the stereotyped view of Copia is a blog called "Digging History" by Sharon Hall, dated 2015.

Sharon accurately states: "Unlike many other western mining towns, Cornucopia was a fairly tame place with only a few killings...." Sharon wrote to me that she may remove the reference to "a few killings" if she cannot find her backup source. That is much closer to the truth than the epidemic of murders at Copia that has been told. Is it "Creepy Copia?" Judge that for yourself.

---

[1] Wikipedia, "Cornucopia Oregon" ("Ghost Town Reputation" section): en.wikipedia.org/wiki/Cornucopia, Oregon.

[2] "This Abandoned Mining Town In Oregon Is Downright Fascinating To Explore," Only In Your State: www.onlyinyourstate.com/oregon/mining-town-or (bottom of webpage).

[3] *Drills and Mills*, self-published ©Will Meyerrieks 2003, page 238.

[4] Madonna Merced, B.O.S.S.: www.stalkingnightshadows.com.

CHAPTER 9

REBIRTH OF CORNUCOPIA

"Used to be the heart of town
Don't tell me this town ain't got no heart
Just gotta poke around"

"Shakedown Street" by The Grateful Dead,
copyright Ice Nine Publishing, 1978

CORNUCOPIA IS UNDERGOING A REBIRTH. FOLLOWING ARE comments from talks with Galen West and Larry Bush. Larry was the lead geologist for Cornucopia Mines from about 1979 to 1982. Galen owns several Copia lots and two historic cabins. Galen's log cabin is where Bob Taylor was born.

Galen West

Galen kindly gave nearly two hours of conversations and two meetings. Galen's great-grandparents and young grandmother came over the Oregon Trail in a covered wagon. They started at the very beginning of the trail at Independence, Missouri. Galen's great-grandparents were farmers and ranchers. His Grandmother spent most of her early days teaching, including at the nearby mining town of Copperfield, Oregon. Galen was a dentist for 33 years and former owner of several Alaska commercial fishing businesses.

Arriving in Copia for the first time in the- mid 1940's, Galen: "My grandfather and father both worked as miners at Cornucopia during various times. Our home is near Halfway. I stay at our Copia [the non-log one] cabin upon occasion. It is one of three original mine built and then mine-owned homes built on the north end of town. Once there were five, two are gone. One was caved in by snow, and the owners converted it into an A frame. Ours is mostly original. It had a stone foundation which we reinforced with concrete. We put a cement floor in the then-dirt basement. We used recycled beams from mine building wreckage to reinforce the floor."

Galen's father's cabin was once broken into by vandals/robbers. His brother owns several lots in Copia, as well as his father's old cabin. Galen's meticulous restoration efforts at his log cabin involve every part of the cabin. Even the new log chinking is made to look old.

In answer to questions about Copia's water system: "The town water sources were springs near and from Elk Creek. This is all on the west side of Pine Creek. The city's residents still own water rights. There was a wooden cistern built around 1895. A newer, smaller, water tank was put in. Our cabin [not the log one] still uses water from the original city water system. The water system is broken for the homes on the east side of Main Street. If any home in that area turns on its water, it quickly drains the whole system due to broken pipe leakage. Our log cabin is not on the city system. We have water there straight out of Elk Creek."

Galen discussed the mine and mine mill buildings: "The Coulter tunnel provided water for the mine to move, along with gravity flow, crushed ore and waste along in the ore milling system. The largest building was the mine mill, four stories high, going downhill in stages. At the beginning was a ball mill [crusher]. There was a lot of machinery in the mill."

Some of the machinery would have been gone due to the mine selling used machinery to other mines, whenever they could. Working for the mine after shutdown, Charlie Sneddon sold as much scrap iron as he could salvage. This helped the mine pay his, Chris Schneider's and Sylvester Marker's salaries after shutdown.

Galen: "There was a covered area one could drive into that was about 100 feet long for turning around, loading and unloading machinery and parts. As a kid, I noticed that the large warehouse, next to the mountain, had a stockroom still with a lot of supplies in it.

Shovels, stuff like that. There was also a commissary for miner's to buy stuff, still nearly full of gear. The drying room and solarium were still there. Inside, it was two stories tall so miners could dry their clothes up above, between shifts.

"I went in the Coulter Adit a couple of times. It was really breezy in there because of air coming in from openings way up the mountain, flowing downward due to Barometric pressure. The tunnel was self-draining [carefully engineered to slightly slope downward]. When I got out, I was all wet from water constantly dripping."

Answering a question about what Chris and Jessie Schneider were like, Galen: "I stayed overnight there a few times. Chris was tall, thin, stoic, disciplined and strict. When he spoke it was well thought out. He was a really nice guy.

"Jessie was small, often had a smile on her face. She liked making jokes, giving two-line sentences that had a humorous twist. She was quick witted. The nicest lady. She had a beautiful lawn and flower garden in front of her house."

Camaraderie is a theme that continually occurs in Cornucopia tales. Religion is sometimes mentioned. Two early photos exist of a church in Copia, one is labeled "Catholic Church." The author made calls to the combined central and eastern Oregon church head-quarters, called the Diocese office, in Baker City. These buildings are a beautiful cut stone complex of church and offices, over 100 years old. During the last call, the church office worker said that there were no records of a church in Copia. She didn't think there ever was a Catholic Church in Cornucopia. Was the Catholic Church ghostly, to the church office?

Answering a question about the denomination of the church in Copia, Galen states: "The church was Catholic. I knew the people who bought it from the county for back taxes. The new owners confirmed that it was Catholic." It seems that the church records of the Copia flock have been lost.

A question about herds of sheep coming through Copia, Galen: "I remember the last time sheep were driven through town towards pastures up Pine Creek. The herd was owned by the Densley family. They would bring the sheep by truck up to a pen on the slum dam, then herd them up the valley to pasture."

Sometime after that, sheep grazing in the Wallowas was stopped by the Forest Service. Sheep grazing was thought to be destructive to the ecology of fragile mountain meadows.

Galen: "There was a very early, barn like, USFS station, north of Halfway. In the mid-1930's, a new station was built. The old ranger station started out west of Halfway. It was moved south to Pine Town, nearby."

Research indicates that it was built by Franklin Roosevelt's New Deal program – the Civilian Conservation Corps. The Forest Service can't confirm either who built their Halfway ranger station, or the date it was built. Government permitting, monitoring of grazing – both cattle and sheep – and logging all around Cornucopia would have been more carefully coordinated by this USFS station beginning in the 1930's.

Finally, Galen mentioned the one of the two Cornucopia bogeymen, forest fire: "I had a gold mining claim up Pine Creek, on the way up to the Simmons Mine area. All my mine development work, a building and mining gear, was burnt in a forest fire.

Larry Bush

Larry lives in Pine Valley. He helped with the second yearly walking tour of Cornucopia. Larry gave pertinent information for the first book about the mine and for this volume. His company almost began a revival of the ghost town in the early 1980's.

"United Nuclear started hiring for mining efforts at Cornucopia in 1981. We started with four people at around $8 to $10 per hour. We built up to 20 workers, many full time, by 1982." That's a very good wage average, at the time, in an area of few jobs.

Larry continues: "The Fountain Store and the mine's 1930's assay building were still there when we started, both now gone. Knocked down by heavy snow by the time we were done. Our new mine building, the down from the Keith Adit was for showers, restrooms, a dry room, geology and engineering departments.

"There were between one and two people who lived in Copia during the winter in the early 1980's. Our maintenance shop [by now looking old and weathered] had track running into it. This was near the Keith Adit, built in 1981. The new adit was cut into the mountain starting in 1981. We named it the 'Keith' – after our CEO. All of our work was called 'mine development.' We never got to the point where we could actually mine gold ore.

"We had no mine maps when we bought the property. I found some detailed maps from Dr. Goodspeed's estate [a teacher at University of Washington who used to take summer geology classes on field trips to Copia] for sale in a bookstore in Washington, and bought them."

The maps were from the mine itself, on linen (vellum), called "grade maps." Most mine records were burnt in a fire.

"We drove the lower adit: The Keith – in 470 feet before we connected to the original 1930's Coulter tunnel. The Coulter was flooded behind a cave-in, tons of water, and would have washed whoever broke through that cave-in [if near the portal] right down to the Snake River.

"We finally reached the 1930's Coulter tunnel. Even then there was quite a bit of water. We had to make new workings around two Coulter tunnel cave-ins. Called 'incompetent rock.' Inside, we found the miner's lunch room at 6,200 feet in." [Author's note: this was an area of the mine that had worked for gold, then further blasted to create the lunchroom in the 1930's to reduce miner travel time from the workings back out to the portal.]

"The lunch room had cemented walls and ceilings, for safety from rock fall. When we stopped clearing and re-timbering, we were just 90 feet from good ore. The ore we saw was in a partly flooded part of the mine."

"Power lines to the mine would have cost between $500,000 and $800,000 due to the distance to the nearest transformer capable for a tie in. That's the lower end of Pine Valley. The nearest smelter that we could of shipped ore to was in British Columbia at the time.

"New management decided that United Nuclear was to step back from all mining efforts. In 1983 UNC stopped funding at Cornucopia because of litigation between companies. The crash [in the mid 1980's] in the gold price did not affect our operations.

"We also completed clean up and covering of the 'slum dam' below the lodge." This effort was graded by both the EPA and USFS as successful – "No Further Action" needed. Larry stated that forest fire danger was a real threat to the town and the mine: "The last major fire at Copia came within one and ½ miles of the town."

By 2008, the town of Copia had been a true empty ghost town for about one half of each year, for 38 years. This number does not count the two years when UNC employees lived in Cornucopia during winter. There were: loggers, summer residents, tourists, hikers, hunters, gold panners, people fishing, ATV riders, and horseback riders coming through Copia from time to time throughout the summers. Some recreationalists visited each winter, snowmobile riders and cross country skiers, even before the lodge.

On a fine early summer 2008 morning, the sun burst through a ridge of the Wallowas, east of Cornucopia. The sun rose from the area above Schneider Meadow, crept down warm and golden through the trees on the west side of the canyon. The sun shone bright and yellow upon the new – about to open for the first time – Cornucopia Lodge.[1] From this day on Copia was no longer a total ghost town during snow times. The lodge staff would live here year-round. There is now a heart of town again in Cornucopia; the lodge. The village of Cornucopia, with the year-round lodge and rental cabins, is open for year-round business once again.

There are now nearly 40 buildings in Copia. This is an approximate count, not counting sheds, but counting all the buildings at Copia pack station and lodge. Many are summer vacation homes. In an informal count of the town's buildings, it looks like a dozen of the buildings are from the late 1930's and earlier.

It is hard to distinguish the age of a remodeled cabin built as a miner's cabin in 1939 and used as a summer cabin. Compare that to cabin built in the early 1950's and also remodeled. It is also difficult to determine the exact age of any of the cabins and homes in Copia, without interviewing each the owners, who are often not at the site.

Commercial or civic historical structures in Copia: the jail, the boarding house and the mine's two cement vaults. Perhaps the miner's cabin that was reportedly used as a brothel should be considered as a commercial structure. Could the jail, combined with the purchase of the boarding house, the purchase of Chris and Jessie Schneider's ornate home, be preserved, and become the basis for a small new three structure State of Oregon Park or a Baker County Park?

As a volunteer for several cumulative weeks, over the years, at La Pine State Park, I know Oregon State Parks have scant funding to maintain what they have. Our Oregon parks rely on volunteers to provide much of their customer service and some maintenance. According to a 2016 article in the *Baker City Herald*, Baker County, like state parks, is also on a very tight budget. There is Oregon lottery funding allocated for future new state parks. Could some of this money be applied to Cornucopia? As the reputation of the beauty of Baker County grows, so will the number of visitors, and the population. The demand for public recreation will also grow.

Why not dream of a basic, very small, Cornucopia State or Baker County Park? I'm not at all thinking of the entire town, nor surrounding lands, nor private cabins. The park could include the as existing disputed Main Street, eliminating the road boundary controversy and provide a small bit of funding for street maintenance. A notion is presented here of preserving three key historical buildings of the town that remain, two of them in danger structurally. The park could also put a sign in front of the vanished Keller Hotel, identifying the largest business in Copia.

Another wild dream would be to have an annual Copia restoration fundraising baseball game on the Fourth of July. Just like in the old days, the game would be played on the Slum Dam. The ball teams could be named: "The Miners vs. The Cowboys/Cowgirls." We could borrow the baseline chalk machine and bases from the school in Halfway. I'd certainly be willing to volunteer serving on a team to set up the field. No holes could be dug for field fence posts. Many used softballs would have to be donated because without fences, lots of balls would be lost.

Fans would bring their own lawn chairs. A museum donation would be requested from each fan and player. The lodge could sell tasty snacks. There would be big fun. With no outfield fence there would be many home runs. A Copia cultural tradition would be continued. "Buy me some peanuts and Crackerjacks…."

The gold miner Boarding House badly needs to be stabilized before snow knocks it down. The boarding house and the former Schneider home are privately owned, but of vital importance for visiting tourists who want to see a few authentic "old west" parts of the town that remain. If nothing happened as far as Baker County or the state, perhaps a benefactor could be found to create some kind of historic group for funding, at least, to stabilize the leaning boarding house.

Will any of historic or even new Copia be left in another hundred years? Survival is still an issue for the town, as it was from the beginning. Will it become a ghost town, again? We hope not! Forest fires, alone, could easily erase the town. Forest fires start earlier in the season, get larger and more frequent each year. Climate change is a real, scary threat to the survival of Cornucopia.

The United States Forest Service allotted 16% of its budget for firefighting in 1996. By 2016, the percentage of the USFS budget spent on firefighting was 54%. The latest fire costs are truly staggering; nearly 2 billion dollars spent in 2016, on national fire suppression efforts alone, by the beleaguered USFS.[2] We all need to be fire conscious; campers, people using any power equipment in the forest, all of us, all the time. Even in a remote gold mining ghost town like Copia.

Visible signs of our restlessness, ghost towns exist throughout the west. Pioneers that became ranchers and farmers sank deep roots. Gold miners tended not to. It is not intended to paint historic Cornucopia as some kind of utopia. The town had its challenges, as any town does.

What remains of this mining town, physically and culturally, is fragmentary. The human treasures at Copia remain, the stories of the last miners and their families, before they passed on. The stories of townspeople that vividly remember the village: Paul, Betty, Blair, Ann and others enrich us. These four citizens of Copia have much in common. They have a golden memory of growing up in a scenic small mountain town and the start from scratch successful arc of their professional lives.

A town's reputation is not cast from only pure metal. Reputations are cast from many kinds of ore. Cornucopia's reputation is not just a hardworking miner and family member tale, nor just a good times town tale, nor a town doomed to die as a ghost town tale. The tale of Cornucopia is an amalgamation of many elements. This includes the current residents, the lodge, the pack station and visitors.

When we visit, let's all appoint ourselves Copia style volunteer Sheriffs and Fire Marshalls. This is needed especially during summer fire season. Go to Halfway and watch the fireworks show instead of setting any fireworks off anywhere near Cornucopia in the summer. That way, the town may survive for a long time. Not much we can do about the other bogeymen, heavy snow loads. We can promote and donate funding for preservation efforts to strengthen the few historic buildings.

Those Wallowas, living mountains making ceaseless geologic interactions, closed the Coulter, Union and Keith mine adits. The mountains are trying to consume the boarding house, to fold it back into the earth. It would be a worthy battle to keep the boarding house standing.

We can extrapolate lessons from Cornucopia; understand ourselves and our nation better. We study the history and the citizens of this tiny gold mining town in the Wallowa Mountains. To look at a true bit of the old Wild West, examine carefully the rugged and hardworking character of the citizens of Copia. It's a bonanza. You will strike gold!

---

[1] Cornucopia Lodge: www.facebook.com/CornucopiaLodge.
[2] USFS: www.fs.fed.us/sites/default/files/2015-Fire-Budget-Report.pdf.

AFTERWORD AND TAILINGS

THREE MEN IN BLACK
AND ONE WOMAN

"I was young on this mountain, now I am old
One night I lay down, and woke up to find
That my childhood was over… I went back down in the mine"

"The Mountain" by Steve Earle, copyright W.B. music, 1995

MY THREE COPIA HIKING PARTNERS AND I HAD NOT MET before. There had been many phone conversations and emailing between us. Our common cause was fundraising to help preserve what's left of Copia, particularly the jail. Before my first talk at Cornucopia Lodge in 2016, we agreed to meet in Copia, in front of the Schneider house. The Gulick's continuing preservation efforts were evident at the home.

Needing to better understand the town, I wanted to give a more accurate presentation for the walking tour. There we were: Dale Taylor and Bob Taylor and myself, three guys named Taylor, by no plan, all arriving in front of the Schneider/Gulick house Copia wearing plain black t-shirts. A museum staffer also accompanied us. What are the odds of that? Three older guys, not in a rock or country band, meeting for the first time, all showed up all wearing black t-shirts. It was spooky, so fitting, for a hike in a ghost town.

During our noodling around in Copia, deep in the woods, we discovered the large mostly buried safe of the Keller Hotel. Not the safe stolen by Six Shooter Carnahan, a mine safe theft described previously. Like the stolen safe, it *was missing its door*. Nothing but forest duff was inside. No gold bar from the Keller bar inside the safe, dang. At the Keller site, Dale discovered a stoved in old blue bucket which he joked was from the Blue Bucket Mine. But this bucket was metal; the one in the 1850's blue bucket legend was wooden. More jokes followed. As always, in the town of Copia, we had a hoot.

A tour of the log cabin was given by Bob Taylor, owned and being carefully restored by Galen West. We admired the jail, in the beginning process of getting a new roof. It was so right of Pine Valley Community Museum to have the original, old roof put back on top of the watertight new roof. This construction method preserved the authentic look of the jail.

At the Cornucopia Lodge's 2016 and 2017 History Talks, we had wonderful discussions about the town. We recognized the need to preserve what remains. After the talks, I hosted guided walking tours of the town. New Copia history details emerged from my co-walkers, both during the 2016 and 2017 history walks.

Bob Taylor helped with the tour. He revealed that he was delivered by the previously discussed Dr. Pollack. Galen West was also delivered by Dr. Pollack in Halfway, in the home that his family still inhabits.

Near the log cabin, two other folks chimed in to the conversation: "I was delivered by Dr. Pollack, too, in Halfway." Then a third person stated: "I was delivered by Dr. Pollack's son, who was a doctor." Another comment: "Dr. Pollack helped my dad save the life of a calf, one time, when we couldn't find a vet." They were having an exclusive impromptu club meeting, right there in the middle of Copia's Main Street, the club named *People delivered by Dr. Pollock or his son, and whose livestock were saved by the Doctor.*

By choosing certain details from Dr. Pollack's book for this volume, the doctor was painted as somewhat of a curmudgeon. He demonstrated that personality trait in many places in his autobiography. Apparently, the Doctor had a kinder side, too.

During the 2017 town tour, Cornucopia Mines Geologist Larry Bush gave fine detail about the geology of the rocks. Larry explained their work drilling into and intercepting the Coulter Adit in the early

1980's. It was an extremely difficult task for UNC to get into the 1930's mine tunnel. Chris Schneider and Charley Sneddon had kept the original adit open after mine closure in 1941.They kept replacing rotting timbers into the 1950's. Not much work in the mine had been done since the 1950's.

When Larry arrived on the job in 1981 the Coulter Adit was caved. The ground at and around the old Coulter cave-in was still unstable. Larry states that the ground around the new adit was unstable, too. By 2017, the 1980 Keith Adit has, like the old Coulter, caved in. Yet another example why it is a very bad, possibly fatal idea to go into old gold mines.

Inside the mountain, these wise 1980's miners, just like the 1930's miners, were careful. Nearly a mile inside the mountain they connected to the old tunnel. Just a few connecting holes were drilled at first. Air was pumped at the deepest part, while they worked inside the mine. Outside, there was a catchment basin to collect the mine water sediments before the newly draining mine water entered Pine Creek.

As we know, the 1980's gold miners encountered two cave-ins inside the Coulter Tunnel. Each time, it was necessary to route a new tunnel around the cave in area, and reconnect to the Coulter Tunnel. No wonder over a half a million dollars was spent before even seeing gold bearing ore. One might think: just open the old mine and simply take out the gold. Mining is not at all that easy, or in any sense inexpensive. Development costs and fulfilling needed environmental rules makes current gold mining very expensive. Let alone the cost of mine mills.

Toxic waste is often a problem with mining mills. A newly found source of information just emerged about Cornucopia Mines. In the first book, it was impossible to verify where the Cornucopia mine related 1920's and 1930's site of Black Butte, Oregon was located. Cornucopia Mines Board of Directors were documented to have met in Black Butte several times. At the time, it could not be determined what the exact connection was between Black Butte and Cornucopia Mines.

At the state of Oregon online Historical Archives, there are several Cornucopia Mines documents newly available. One is called "1937 Annual Report."[1] It is signed by Cornucopia Mines Vice President Frank Taylor. No relation to Dale or Bob Taylor's or my families. The documents reference the mine board of directors meetings in "Blackbutte" (their spelling) Oregon. Not the central Oregon mountain and 1960's resort near Sisters.

We now know that Blackbutte, also spelled Black Butte, was a town, totally gone, near the Bohemia Mining area east of Cottage Grove in western Oregon. Confusingly, the alternative spelling of the mine and the town is the same as Black Butte Resort. The documents state that the main business in Blackbutte, or Black Butte, was a mercury mine. The mine and mill were upstream from Cottage Grove Reservoir. The Cornucopia Mines Company bought mercury from the Blackbutte Mine for their gold ore milling process in Cornucopia.

Several documents indicate that Cornucopia Mines was deeply involved with the Blackbutte Mercury Mine. The mine and mine mill in western Oregon were owned by "The Quicksilver Syndicate." Sounds like a rock band. The primary stock holder of the syndicate was Robert Betts. Betts was the primary stockholder for many years of the Cornucopia Mines Company.

Remember the Cornucopia Mines site has an EPA – Environmental Protection Agency – superfund designation of "N.F.A."- no further action necessary. Trout now exist in Pine Creek.

Unfortunately, the western Oregon Black Butte site is an active EPA superfund site. A site needing ongoing taxpayer funded environmental mitigation. It is planned to continue the mine mill waste clean-up. There is a recommendation that no one eat any bass taken from downstream Cottage Grove Reservoir due to mercury contamination. The eating of trout from the reservoir is recommended only for recently planted hatchery trout, not for larger, older, trout.[2] When trout are caught at Cottage Grove Reservoir, you have to ask the trout how old it is before you eat it. In order to ask, learning trout language would be a challenge.

Using mercury for their gold milling process in Eastern Oregon, Cornucopia Mines was doing nothing at all unusual. Gold mines throughout the west extensively used mercury in the mine ore milling process, especially pre-1920's. In 1936 Cornucopia Mines built a new floatation process mill. The new mill recovered 90% of the gold from the ore. This was unlike the 40 to 60% gold recovery that the mercury only process produced. The pre 1930's mercury and cyanide milling process recovered more gold than the mercury process alone. It is very expensive for the mine to purchase cyanide for the floatation process, to begin with. So, cyanide is recovered as much as possible. This new mill floatation process was designed considering that cyanide quickly dissipates in the waste materials.

Mercury mine milling process always leaves a large amount of mercury laden toxic waste behind. Clean up, including treating underground water, is lengthy and expensive. One tiny ghostly mystery, from the first book – "where is Black Butte, and why did the Cornucopia Mines Board meet there once in a while?" – has been solved.

To some, it's currently popular to denigrate the EPA, even wanting to eliminate it. Yet EPA federal funding was very helpful in solving ecological problems at the Slum Dam at Copia. If cleanup efforts continue, we may be able to eat Bass and older trout from Cottage Grove Reservoir. Sport fishing, such a big recreational industry in Oregon, helps our economy. Some tourists come to Cornucopia to hike up Pine Valley and fish.

In Copia is the site of the historic Cornucopia Mine's Donley Recreation Center. A large cement slab foundation remains. The site of the center is also about one quarter mile north of the site of Keller's Dance Hall, both were on Main Street.

In the tradition of Keller Dance Hall and Donley Recreation Hall, music, dancing and other events continue at the yearly Cornucopia Arts Council's "Pine Fest." The fest is held in early September at the Halfway Fairgrounds. Just like in the two vanished Copia recreation venues: Americana style music, beer, wine and good times are served. The Pine Fest won a statewide award for "Best Music Festival" in 2016. We like to have our cultural history preserved and presented. Events like the Halfway music festival help continue the traditions of Cornucopia.

In 2017, the real estate company, based back east, "Hilco" sold the Copia mine property. Over 800 acres including historic and newer buildings, and some of the town were sold together. A web page describes the company. There was a brief description of their Cornucopia real estate listing.

No one interviewed, who lived in Cornucopia, ever mentioned poor customer service in town. I asked several what it was like inside the Copia stores, getting the idea that the Copia ethos of friendliness and helpfulness was always present. It is very plausible to assume that customer service provided by the stores, saloons, recreation centers and other retail businesses in Cornucopia was positive and helpful.

Over several weeks, seven unreturned phone messages were left at Hilco Real Estate. My name and number was clearly left each time, politely asking for contact. I did not identify myself as a writer or a real estate investor, although that's true, at times.

Hilco Reality offered a classic example of poor customer service. The service given by Hilco makes me feel even better about repeated visits as a happy customer to businesses like Cornucopia Lodge, Les Schwab and Nordstrom. These businesses provide outstanding customer service.

On my eighth effort someone picked up at the mysterious Hilco number. This somewhat curt answering service staffer would not disclose the price for mine lands and buildings. He refused to connect me with a supervisor. This staffer seemed somewhat upset to have to talk to me. He seemed to want to get rid of me as soon as possible. I was not asking history questions, just to be able to reach a real estate agent and find out the asking price. More than two weeks after my last call, one of the Hilco realtors did finally return my call. They would not state even an opening or ballpark price for their Copia listing. All my interactions with Hilco were....ghostly.

Another Copia related example of, to put it in a somewhat neutral term – less than prosaic – customer service follows. This was exemplified by my numerous attempts to get two basic questions answered by the United States Forest Service. I simply wanted to know the year that the USFS started the Halfway Ranger Station, and who built it. The new (at the time) ranger station clearly had an effect on Cornucopia. We know that at one time there were several depression era Civilian Conservation Corps – CCC – buildings built at Halfway Ranger Station. We know that USFS hired its first female employee in the Wallowas, Freda Martin, in about 1942. Freda was multi-talented: she built trails, fought fires, panned for gold, and was a skilled hunter-taxidermist.

Meanwhile, six calls, four weeks passing, four messages left on answering machines with three USFS Baker City headquarters employees. Two of the messages were left for Baker City based trained USFS archeologists. These staffers should have been able to easily answer my two brief historical questions.

No answers, no returned calls. I expressed my frustration about the Baker City USFS headquarters with the Halfway USFS staffer. None of my calls were being returned. It was suggested she might send my questions to her USFS supervisor. My phone number and email were repeated. A new-fangled gadget called email comes to mind as a way to help this customer. The staffer abruptly closed the conversation by stating that she was soon closing the Halfway station early for the year. I was advised that I should resume my quest next summer.

Five weeks after the first attempt, a staffer called from USFS Wallowa-Whitman headquarters in Baker City. She stated that the USFS did not know when they started its station in Halfway, or who built it. She gave me the names of two local citizens of Halfway who might know. End of story. Let's give the overworked USFS a break. They were busy fighting forest fires for much of the summer. Heroic firefighters.

The summer 2017 Cornucopia Lodge history talk was called "Three Celebrations." Copia's biggest mining days celebrations were Labor Day and the Fourth of July. My history talk was also a celebration of the former ghost town of Cornucopia's 132nd birthday. Really, a celebration of the rebirth of the town, having once been a ghost town – in winter – for nearly 40 years, now no longer. Despite the dispute over the year that the town was founded, we can celebrate the rich cultural history and beauty of Cornucopia whenever we choose.

At the history talk, lodge and pack station owner David Moore announced that he and his wife Katherine were the buyers of the entire Cornucopia Mines lands and buildings. Over the next few years, recreational opportunities will be improved on the mine lands. New horseback, hiking, cross country skiing and snowmobile trails are in the planning stages. David emphasized the apt warning to stay totally away from all old mine workings and buildings.

The mine lands bought have no improvements, are all private, and are closed for safety reasons. Special permission is required to visit the recently bought lands. This large, local purchase should have a positive effect on preserving what remains at Copia. After all, a giant corporation owning ski resorts and condos could have bought and radically changed the upper part of Pine Valley forever. A September 2016 article in the *Baker City Herald* stated that, with the current price of gold, a total of $406 million worth of gold has been taken from Cornucopia Mines.

We all hope that what is left of the town will still be preserved for another 130 years. Only our grandchildren or great grandchildren will know. If the lodge is still there, it will be an antique grand old hotel. Could we somehow find out in the future if the village lasted into the next century? If any of us could possibly manage to communicate in some minute way with our future families; in a dream, or a spiritual way. Perhaps we'll know, or perhaps not, about the future of the boom and ghost town of Cornucopia. Time will tell.

---

[1]   Oregon   Historical   Society   Website: librarycatalog.ohs.org/EOSWebOPAC/OPAC/Search/SimpleSearch.aspx
[2] Oregon Fishing Forum - www.oregonfishingforum.com/forum/fishing-by-location/fishing-in-willamette-zone/2691-cottage-grove-reservoir.

APPENDIX

Remaining Oregon Gold Miner Boarding Houses

THERE ARE ONE OR TWO MORE MINE BOARDING HOUSES IN Oregon, not in ruins, that the author has not been to, not on the list below. Photos exist of one, the location not disclosed. Order of list is best preserved first:

* Jawbone Flats boarding house. About 60 miles east of Salem. A one hour walk or 30 minute mountain bike ride past locked gate, not private land. One can rent this boarding house, and gold miner cabins from the Opal Creek (Jawbone Flats) educational conservancy that maintains this well-preserved

mining village. Staff will drive down and pick you up at the gate if you are renting one of the miner cabins or the boarding house.

* Buffalo Mine boarding house. North of Granite in the Cable Cove area on private land. Don't visit, stay away, unless mine ownership has changed and you are able to get specific permission to visit in advance. I'm told that someone on the property shoots over the heads of fools who go past the "No Trespassing" sign. Especially do not go there if you are very tall.

* Helena Mine boarding house. Bohemia Mines district, east of Cottage Grove. On private land, also posted no trespassing. I obtained permission; please don't bother the mine owners. The two story boarding house is girdled by a thick logging cable, holding it to the mountain. This cable prevents snow from knocking the large boarding house over. The boarding house is occupied for most of each summer, not open for tours. The last time I visited, the owners were engaged in logging on their property.

* Argonaut Mine house. North of Granite, Fruit Creek area. Four wheel drive access only. Situated on what is now public land. The boarding looks like a house with kitchen, dining room and large room for miner beds. All windows are gone, some snow damage inside. The building was in surprisingly good condition, eight years ago.

* Cornucopia Mines boarding house. You can find it, but don't go in.

* Roberts Mine boarding house. Five mile south west of ghost town of Greenhorn. Four wheel drive access only. Large, dangerous two story log house in semi-ruins.

REFERENCE SOURCES

Pine Valley Community Museum, 115 E Record Street, Halfway, OR 97834.

A Pictorial History of Gold Mining in the Blue Mountains of Eastern Oregon, Howard Brooks, Baker County Historical Society, 2007 (no ISBN given). .

Outlaw Tales of Oregon, Jim Yuskavitch, Globe Pequot Press, 2007. ISBN 978-0-7627-7263-6.

University of Oregon, Knight Library, Oregon Collection: 2 boxes of ledgers and letters, records from Cornucopia Mines.

University of Utah, Marriott Library, Box 35 XOP, FD #s 16 and 17.

Author's collection of 100 timecards, requisitions and shift reports by Cornucopia Mines, 1937 to 1940.

Gold Mining in Oregon, Bert Webber, 1995. Webb Research Publishers. ISBN 0-936738-77-4.

Oregon's Golden Years, Miles F. Potter 1976. Caxton Printers. ISBN 0-87004-254-8.

Numerous posted online newspaper articles: *Baker City Herald*, various dates.

Oregon State Department of Geology and Minerals, H. Brooks and L. Ramp, state of Oregon publication, 1968. No ISBN provided.

Ghost Towns of the Pacific Frontier, Lambert Florin, 1970. Promontory Press. ISBN # 0 -88394068 x.

Baker County Library District (Oregon) Digital Archive of Historic Photographs - bakeroregonhistory.info/exhibit2/e20121b.htm

The Mining Camps Speak, Beth and Bill Sagstetter, 1998. Self-Published. ISBN 0-9645824-1-4.

Last Call: The Rise and Fall of Prohibition, Daniel Okrent. 2010, Scribner. ISBN 978-0-7432-7702-0.

The Cornucopia: Oregon's Richest Gold Mine, Thomas T. Cook, 2016. Createspace. ISBN 978-1523330768.

ABOUT THE AUTHOR

Thomas Cook's articles have appeared in publications such as Roseburg, Oregon's *News Review.* This is his second book, after *The Cornucopia: Oregon's Richest Gold Mine.* He is a retired educator and counselor living in Eugene and La Pine, Oregon.

**For current preservation efforts at Cornucopia,
please send donations to:**

Cornucopia Fund
Pine Valley Community Museum
P.O. Box 673
Halfway, Oregon 97834

Praise for Thomas T. Cook's *The Cornucopia, Oregon's Richest Gold Mine:*

"In *The Cornucopia*, Tom Cook leads us on an expedition 100 years back in time to a remote mountainside in Northeast Oregon. Once there, Cook lets us experience the enchanting, dangerous and sometimes heartwarming history of Oregon's largest gold mining operation. Not fanciful fiction, this is an affectionately told story of real people scratching a living out of the cold hard rock of Oregon's Wallowa Mountains. *The Cornucopia* adds a new volume to the great historical literature about America's Old West."

- Dave Imus, author of *The Essential Geography of the United States of America* and other maps

"Thomas Cook captures the wonder and the hardship of the Cornucopia, and the tumultuous history of the region."

- James E. Meacham, author and director of University of Oregon InfoGraphics Laboratory

Made in the USA
Monee, IL
25 September 2023

43384655R00075